PAKISTAN (
A STUDY OF DICHOTOMIES
AND CHALLENGES

MAKHDOOM SHAHAB-UD-DIN

AURAQ
PUBLICATIONS

Printed: November, 2023   Editor: Abdul Rehman
Edition: 1st   Cover Design: Iqbal Hussain Rizvi
ISBN: 978-969-749-268-8
Price: Rs 1600 PKR, $12 US

AURAQ
PUBLICATIONS

www.auraqpublications.com | raabta@auraqpublications.com
@AuraqPublications | @AuraqBooks | +92-300-0571-530
Printed and Bound by *Passive Printers* - www.passiveprinters.com

DEDICATION

This book is dedicated to the resilient spirit and unwavering courage of the 250 million people of Pakistan, whose hopes and dreams are the ink that writes the country's future

CONTENTS

1. INTRODUCTION

1.1 PAKISTAN UNVEILED: AN OVERVIEW

The Islamic Republic of Pakistan, a land steeped in rich history and diverse cultures, presents a fascinating paradox. Established in 1947 with a vision of prosperity and unity, the nation is now home to over 220 million inhabitants, making it the world's fifth-most populous country. Its geopolitical position at the crossroads of South, Central, and West Asia confers upon it a strategic significance in global affairs. Yet, despite having a wealth of natural resources and a resilient populace, the path to prosperity for Pakistan has been fraught with trials that the country continues to grapple with. Pakistan's journey presents a complex interplay of triumphs and challenges – a true paradox, a puzzle that this book aims to unravel.

1.2 PURPOSE AND SCOPE OF THE BOOK

"Pakistan Unveiled: A Study of Dichotomies and Challenges" embarks on a journey into the heart of Pakistan's story, highlighting the trials it has faced and the triumphs it has achieved. It aims to illuminate the myriad complexities underpinning the country's socio-political, economic, and cultural fabric. The book does not claim to provide a cure-all solution to Pakistan's problems. Instead, it offers an enlightening perspective on the past, a comprehensive understanding of the present, and a hopeful gaze towards the future.

2. HISTORICAL BACKGROUND

2.1 PRE-PARTITION ERA AND THE BIRTH OF PAKISTAN

The Indian Subcontinent under British Colonial Rule

The genesis of the Pakistani paradox begins not within the geographical confines of modern-day Pakistan, but within the larger framework of the Indian subcontinent under British colonial rule. It was an era of profound socio-economic and political change that set the stage for the events leading to the birth of Pakistan.

In the early 17th century, the East India Company, a British trading firm, set foot on the shores of the Indian subcontinent. Under the guise of trade, the company gradually expanded its influence, ushering in an era of economic exploitation and political subjugation. By the mid-19th century, the Company had assumed control over large swathes of the subcontinent, replacing local rulers and imposing British systems of administration, education, and law. The relentless extraction of resources and the imposition of alien rule created a simmering discontent among the native population, culminating in the Revolt of 1857.

Often termed India's 'First War of Independence,' the Revolt of 1857 was a watershed moment in the history of the subcontinent. It was a violent and bloody uprising against British rule by a wide cross-section of Indian society. Despite its ultimate failure, the revolt was a significant turning point. It marked the end of the East India Company's rule and the beginning of direct governance by the British Crown, known as the Raj.

Under the Raj, the Indian subcontinent experienced profound changes. British policies further entrenched the economic exploitation of the region, disrupting traditional industries and agriculture, leading to widespread poverty and famine. However, alongside this economic turmoil, the British also introduced modern infrastructure, such as railways, telegraph, and postal services, which paradoxically facilitated communication and the exchange of ideas, sowing the seeds of nationalism among the native population.

The British policy of 'Divide and Rule' further impacted the socio-political fabric of the subcontinent. Perhaps the most glaring example of this was the division of Bengal in 1905, a move ostensibly undertaken for administrative efficiency but widely seen as an attempt to fracture the burgeoning nationalist movement along religious lines. This partition incited widespread protests and was ultimately annulled in 1911, but it left a deep-seated communal discord in its wake.

Thus, the British colonial rule, characterized by economic exploitation, political subjugation, and divisive policies, ignited the spark of nationalism in the Indian subcontinent. This period marked the emergence of significant socio-political movements, the rise of influential parties, and the start of the complex journey that would eventually lead to the partition of the subcontinent and the creation of Pakistan. As we delve further into this journey, we must keep in mind the profound impact of these colonial roots, as they continue to influence the trials and triumphs of Pakistan today.

Rise of Nationalist Movements and the Emergence of Two Major Parties

As British colonial rule persisted, a wave of nationalist sentiment began to sweep the Indian subcontinent. Sparked by oppressive policies, divisive tactics, and economic hardships, this led to the emergence of two prominent political entities that would play vital roles in the trajectory of the subcontinent: the Indian National Congress (INC) and the All-India Muslim League (AIML).

Established in 1885, the INC was initially composed of elite, English-educated Indians seeking to obtain a greater political voice within the existing British framework. However, as time passed, the party evolved to reflect broader nationalist sentiments, advocating for Swaraj or self-rule. The Congress successfully mobilized diverse social groups, including peasants, workers, and middle-class intellectuals, unifying them under the banner of Indian nationalism. Nevertheless, its composition, largely perceived as Hindu-majority, created apprehensions amongst the Muslim minority about the protection of their socio-political interests.

In contrast, the AIML was founded in 1906 as a direct response to these growing Muslim anxieties. The party's primary aim was to safeguard and promote the rights of Muslims within the political sphere, which they believed the INC was neglecting. The AIML started as a platform for dialogue between the Muslim community and the British government, gradually transitioning into a powerful voice for the demand for a separate Muslim state.

The Lucknow Pact of 1916 marked a significant milestone in the relations between the INC and the AIML. It saw the two parties reaching a mutual agreement for the first time, advocating for greater Indian autonomy from British rule. The pact also recognized separate electorates for Muslims, reinforcing their political representation. It was seen as a potential turning point for Hindu-Muslim unity.

Moreover, the INC's call for Purna Swaraj (complete

independence) at the Lahore session in 1929 alienated many Muslim leaders. They feared that a united India under Hindu-majority rule would marginalize Muslims and neglect their interests. These fears were not entirely unfounded, given the increasing sway of hardline Hindu nationalist elements within the INC.

This deepening rift between the INC and the AIML, and the growing communal discord, set the stage for the consolidation of the Two-Nation Theory. It also solidified the AIML's demand for a separate nation where Muslims could safeguard their socio-political and cultural interests. Thus, the rise of these two major parties, born out of the crucible of British colonial rule, would play a pivotal role in the formation of modern-day Pakistan. As we explore this journey, I recognize that the triumphs and trials of Pakistan cannot be separated from the complex history of the nationalist movements that led to its creation.

Two-Nation Theory and Demand for a Separate Muslim State

The widening schism between the Indian National Congress and the All-India Muslim League, coupled with the escalating communal tension in the Indian subcontinent, led to the crystallization of the Two-Nation Theory and the consequent demand for a separate Muslim state.

The concept of the Two-Nation Theory emerged from a profound concern among Indian Muslims over the perceived domination of the Hindu majority. With Muslim identity under threat in post-1857 India, Sir Syed Ahmed Khan laid the intellectual groundwork for the idea of separate Muslim nationhood in India. With their distinct cultural, religious, and social identities, he believed that Muslims in India needed to work towards their educational and socio-political upliftment to safeguard their rights and interests in a predominantly Hindu-majority country. The theory later came into its own, going further to present the idea that Hindus and Muslims—with their distinct traditions, languages, and customs—each deserved a separate homeland to preserve and foster their unique religious, cultural, and social identities.

This theory began to gain momentum in the early 20th century, but it was only in the 1930s and 1940s, under the leadership of key figures like Allama Iqbal and Muhammad Ali Jinnah, that it became the foundation for the creation of Pakistan.

Allama Iqbal, a philosopher, poet, and politician, is often considered the spiritual founder of Pakistan. In his presidential address to the AIML in 1930, he proposed the idea of a separate Muslim state in the northwestern regions of India. He argued that Islam offered a comprehensive system of life, distinct from other religious or social systems, and as such, Muslims constituted a nation of their own.

However, it was Muhammad Ali Jinnah, the leader of the AIML, who converted this ideological proposition into a political reality. Initially, Jinnah had advocated for Hindu-Muslim unity, believing that communal harmony was essential for the fight against British rule. But over time, disenchanted with the INC's perceived disregard for Muslim interests, he became a staunch advocate for the Two-Nation Theory.

The Lahore Resolution passed in the AIML's annual session in 1940, was a pivotal moment in this journey. Often referred to as the 'Pakistan Resolution,' it demanded the creation of "independent states" for Muslims in the northwestern and eastern regions of India where they were in the majority. The resolution didn't explicitly mention 'Pakistan,' but it was the first formal articulation of the demand for what would eventually become Pakistan.

The idea of partition faced stiff opposition, not only from the

British and the INC but also from within the Muslim community. However, the political and communal climate in the ensuing years — marked by events like the Quit India Movement, the Rajagopalachari Formula, and the Simla Conference — further cemented the belief among many Muslims that their rights could only be secured in a separate nation.

Thus, the Two-Nation Theory and the demand for a separate Muslim state were not simply born out of a desire for political power. They were the culmination of a complex historical process marked by communal tension, political disagreements, and the profound fear among Muslims of being marginalized in a Hindu-majority India. The birth of Pakistan, the physical manifestation of these theories and demands, marked a radical shift in the subcontinent's history and set the stage for the challenges and triumphs that the nascent state would face in the years to come.

Partition Plan and the Birth of Pakistan

As the clamour for independence grew louder and communal tensions escalated, the idea of partitioning the Indian subcontinent became increasingly inevitable. The concluding years of British colonial rule witnessed intense negotiations, culminating in the acceptance of the partition plan and the birth of a new nation — Pakistan.

In the aftermath of World War II, the British government weakened and facing growing unrest in India, decided to expedite the process of granting independence to the Indian subcontinent. The question of how to accommodate the Muslim demand for a separate nation became pivotal. The appointment of Lord Mountbatten as the last Viceroy of India in 1947 marked a decisive turn in these negotiations.

Mountbatten, after extensive discussions with Indian leaders, proposed a partition plan. Known as the Mountbatten Plan, it outlined the division of British India into two dominions, India, and Pakistan, with the princely states free to choose their allegiance. While it was met with resistance, the urgency to avoid a potential civil war led the Indian National Congress and the All-India Muslim League to reluctantly accept the proposal. The British Parliament passed the Indian Independence Act on July 18, 1947, giving legal sanction to the partition plan.

On August 14, 1947, Pakistan was born. It consisted of two non-contiguous wings, East Pakistan (modern-day Bangladesh) and West Pakistan, separated by a vast expanse of Indian territory. Muhammad Ali Jinnah was appointed as the Governor-General and Liaquat Ali Khan became the first Prime Minister. In his inaugural speech, Jinnah expressed his vision of Pakistan as a democratic state where "Hindus would cease to be Hindus and Muslims would cease to be Muslims, not in the religious sense because that is the personal faith of each individual, but in the political sense as citizens of the State."

However, the birth of Pakistan was accompanied by one of the largest and bloodiest mass migrations in human history. The hastily drawn Radcliffe Line, named after Sir Cyril Radcliffe, who was tasked with demarcating the boundaries, led to confusion and conflict. Approximately 14-16 million people crossed the newly formed borders in both directions, Hindus and Sikhs moving towards India, and Muslims towards Pakistan. The violence that erupted took a heavy toll, with estimates of casualties ranging from several hundred thousand to two million.

The nascent state faced monumental challenges — handling the refugee crisis, settling political structures, grappling with economic hardships, and building a national identity. Despite these hurdles, the creation of Pakistan marked a significant chapter in world history. It was the realization of the dream of millions of Muslims who had strived for a homeland where they could live according to their cultural and religious values.

The birth of Pakistan itself embodies a paradox — a moment of triumph and jubilation, yet also a time of immense suffering and sacrifice. As we trace the trajectory of Pakistan's history, it is important to remember these foundational moments that have shaped the nation's journey, informing its trials, triumphs, and the road to success.

Conclusion: Reflections on the Dawn of a New Nation

The birth of Pakistan in 1947 was a monumental moment, not just in the history of the Indian subcontinent, but in the annals of global history. It marked the successful culmination of a demand for a separate homeland, driven by a unique amalgamation of political, religious, and cultural motivations. At the dawn of this new nation, a sense of optimism and aspiration was palpable among its people. Despite the numerous challenges that lay ahead, the creation of Pakistan represented the triumph of a dream, the actualization of the Two-Nation Theory, and the beginning of a journey toward self-determination.

However, the dawn of this new nation was overshadowed by the immense human tragedy that accompanied the partition of British India. The joy of independence was marred by the suffering endured during one of the largest mass migrations in human history, leading to a long-lasting impact on the socio-cultural fabric of the subcontinent.

Reflecting on the birth of Pakistan is to appreciate the paradox of its existence. Born amidst trials, its history is a testament to resilience and aspiration, setting the stage for the journey of a nation striving to overcome its challenges and achieve its envisioned success.

2.2 POST-PARTITION CHALLENGES AND TRIUMPHS

The birth of Pakistan, while a monumental achievement, was accompanied by a plethora of challenges. Pakistan, now responsible for its governance and future, had to navigate a range of issues, from political to economic, from demographic to social. However, despite these trials, the newly independent nation also experienced several triumphs, testifying to its resilience and determination.

Handling the Refugee Crisis

The aftermath of the partition of India and Pakistan in 1947 triggered a mass migration unparalleled in modern history. The hastily drawn Radcliffe Line, signifying the new borders, led to massive upheaval. Muslims in India moved towards Pakistan, while Hindus and Sikhs in Pakistan crossed the border into India. An estimated 14-16 million people were displaced during this period, and the newly formed nation of Pakistan was tasked with accommodating around 7 million of these refugees.

This mass influx of people represented one of the earliest and most formidable challenges Pakistan faced as a new nation. These refugees, having left everything behind, arrived in their new homeland with hopes of a safe and secure future. The Pakistani government, still nascent and grappling with numerous post-independence issues, had the arduous task of providing immediate relief and long-term rehabilitation to these millions.

Temporary refugee camps sprouted up across the country, particularly in urban centres like Karachi and Lahore, where most refugees were headed. Public buildings, including schools, colleges, and even prisons, were converted into makeshift accommodations. However, these arrangements were grossly inadequate, leading to appalling living conditions marked by overcrowding, lack of sanitation, and scarcity of food. The lack of a robust administrative structure and the paucity of resources added to the magnitude of the crisis. The delivery of basic services such as healthcare was severely hampered, leading to outbreaks of diseases like cholera and malaria. The trauma of displacement was compounded by these living conditions, leading to severe psychological distress among the refugees.

Despite these seemingly insurmountable challenges, the handling of the refugee crisis also showcased the remarkable resilience of the Pakistani people. There were numerous instances of ordinary citizens, themselves struggling with the effects of independence, stepping forward to aid the refugees. Communities opened their homes to displaced families, shared their resources, and provided emotional support to their traumatized brethren. It was a time of shared suffering, but also a demonstration of shared strength and community spirit.

The government, with international aid and domestic efforts, gradually began rehabilitating the refugees. Vacant homes left by Hindus and Sikhs migrating to India were allocated to refugee families. Job programs were launched to provide employment opportunities, and efforts were made to integrate the refugees into the social and cultural fabric of the country.

In retrospect, the refugee crisis of 1947 was one of the first significant trials for Pakistan as a new nation. It was a daunting challenge, one that brought immense suffering and hardship. Yet, it was also during this crisis that the fledgling nation exhibited remarkable resilience and community spirit. It set the stage for the formation of a collective national identity, forged in the crucible of shared trials and tribulations. The manner in which Pakistan handled the refugee crisis became a testament to its ability to navigate adversity, marking an important chapter in its journey towards nationhood.

Establishment of Political Structures

One of the most pivotal challenges for Pakistan post-partition was the establishment of political structures. The nation, now an independent entity, had to build a governance mechanism from scratch. Inherited from the British colonial rule was a political framework, but this needed to be restructured to accommodate the unique socio-political dynamics of Pakistan.

At the core of the governance challenge was the formulation of a constitution that would serve as the blueprint for the nation's political future. Pakistan, with its diverse ethnic and linguistic groups and the overarching aim to embody Islamic values within a democratic framework, faced a complex task in drafting its constitution.

In 1949, just two years after independence, Pakistan's Constituent Assembly passed the Objectives Resolution. Proposed by Prime Minister Liaquat Ali Khan, this resolution served as a foundational document for the constitutional laws of Pakistan. It declared that sovereignty over the entire universe belongs to Allah alone and that the state of Pakistan shall exercise its powers within the limits prescribed by Him. The resolution also emphasized democracy, freedom, equality, tolerance, and social justice, as enshrined in Islam.

However, the journey from this resolution to a formal constitution was fraught with political tensions, power struggles, and disagreements. It took nine years and two Constituent Assemblies for the Constitution to be finally adopted in 1956, marking Pakistan's transition from a dominion to an Islamic Republic. The Constitution enshrined federalism with a parliamentary form of government, fundamental rights, and the principle of the supremacy of law, reflecting the democratic aspirations of its people. However, the journey of constitutional development in Pakistan was just beginning and would see multiple iterations in the years to come.

Another critical aspect of establishing political structures was the creation of administrative systems at the federal, provincial, and local levels. With a dual system of administration inherited from the British - the provinces and the princely states - Pakistan had to develop a system that could integrate these diverse entities.

Despite facing significant political instability and frequent changes in leadership, Pakistan gradually developed its administrative machinery. Key institutions, such as the Election Commission of Pakistan and the Supreme Court, were established. In the provinces, administrative divisions were created, each headed by a commissioner and further divided into districts.

However, political instability, frequent military interventions, and changes in leadership have often disrupted the development and maturation of political structures in Pakistan. Despite these challenges, the nation has consistently strived towards democratic governance.

In retrospect, the establishment of political structures was a mammoth task for post-partition Pakistan. Despite numerous challenges and setbacks, significant strides were made. This period marked a critical phase in Pakistan's political journey, reflecting its aspiration to develop a democratic governance model within the framework of its Islamic identity. As we further delve into the triumphs and trials of Pakistan's journey, it is essential to understand these early political developments, which significantly influenced the nation's future course.

Economic Hurdles and Development

In the aftermath of partition, Pakistan faced an uphill battle in terms of its economic stability and growth. A weak industrial base, agricultural disruption, and the division of assets with India were significant challenges that confronted the newly formed nation.

Pakistan inherited only a small portion of the undivided India's industrial base, and what it did receive was primarily oriented towards the domestic market. The partition resulted in a sharp disruption of the market networks, and most of the jute and cotton production areas, which were the mainstay of the region's economy, were now separated from the processing industries. This further complicated the economic scenario.

Agriculture, the backbone of Pakistan's economy, faced a substantial setback as the migration during partition led to a significant loss of skilled farmers. Additionally, the initial absence of a sound infrastructure, including transport and irrigation facilities, presented substantial hurdles in agricultural development.

The division of assets between India and Pakistan was a complex and contentious issue. A considerable delay in the transfer of funds and assets from India led to a shortage of resources, severely affecting the economic stability of the country. Pakistan had to start virtually from scratch, with low foreign reserves and a limited capacity for revenue collection.

In response to these challenges, Pakistan undertook a series of measures aimed at stimulating economic growth. It launched five-year plans, modeled after the Soviet Union's approach to economic development. These plans targeted critical sectors like agriculture, industry, education, and health, aiming to provide a systematic roadmap for Pakistan's economic progress.

The 1960s marked a turning point in Pakistan's economic journey. Known as the decade of development, this period saw significant industrial and agricultural growth. The Green Revolution, which introduced high-yield crop varieties and modern farming techniques, led to a substantial increase in agricultural production. Industrial policies that encouraged private sector participation led to growth in industries such as textiles, which played a critical role in job creation and export earnings.

The government also sought international aid and entered economic partnerships to bolster its economy. These included agreements with the United States and other Western nations, which provided much-needed economic and military aid during the early years of Pakistan's formation.

However, these developments were not without their shortcomings. Economic disparities between East and West Pakistan were a persistent issue, eventually playing a part in the secession of East Pakistan in 1971. The rapid industrialization also led to an increase in income inequality, and the benefits of the Green Revolution were not equally distributed.

In summary, the economic journey of Pakistan in its early years was marked by significant hurdles but also commendable resilience. Despite the myriad of challenges, the country made significant strides towards economic development and growth. As we further explore the triumphs and trials in Pakistan's path to success, the economic journey offers valuable insights into the nation's adaptive strategies and enduring spirit.

Social Reformation and Education

Emerging as a nascent nation, Pakistan faced myriad social and educational challenges, necessitating comprehensive social reform and the prioritization of education. The fusion of diverse ethnic, linguistic, and religious communities into a cohesive social fabric was a formidable task, coupled with the necessity to enhance literacy and create an educated populace capable of driving the nation's progress.

Social Reformation

At the heart of the social reformation in Pakistan was the quest to navigate its unique identity – a nation carved out of British India, with the aim to provide a homeland for Muslims, yet home to a multi-ethnic and multi-religious population. Balancing the preservation of cultural diversity with the desire for national unity was a critical challenge.

The initial years witnessed attempts to homogenize the culture, primarily through the imposition of Urdu as the national language. This led to discontent among various ethnic groups, especially in East Pakistan, where Bengali was the dominant language. Over time, the government had to recognize the importance of linguistic and cultural diversity and reassess its policies accordingly.

Reformations were needed in many other social domains too. For instance, the patriarchal nature of the society and the stringent tribal and feudal customs led to gender inequality and the marginalization of women. The government took steps towards women's emancipation, including the passage of the Muslim Family Laws Ordinance in 1961, which brought significant reforms in family laws and aimed to protect women's rights.

The government also grappled with reforming harsh feudal and tribal customs, such as "vani" (compensation marriage) and "karo-kari" (honour killings). Efforts were made to legally ban such practices and bring about social awareness. Despite resistance from certain factions, these social reforms marked the beginnings of a long and ongoing journey towards a more egalitarian society.

Education

Education was another major arena that required immediate attention. At independence, Pakistan had a low literacy rate, with a vast majority of the population having no access to formal education. The government recognized education as a vital tool for national development and social upliftment, leading to the institution of several reforms and initiatives.

The first educational conference held in Karachi in 1947 underscored the need for a uniform system of education, emphasizing free and compulsory education for all children. The government established public schools and universities, such as the University of Karachi (1951) and Quaid-i-Azam University (1967), to increase access to education.

Technical and vocational training programs were also initiated to equip the youth with practical skills. Madrasa education reform was another area of focus, aimed at integrating religious schools into the mainstream education system by introducing modern subjects alongside religious studies.

The education sector did face numerous hurdles. Lack of infrastructure, insufficient funding, and a shortage of trained teachers were significant challenges. Disparities in education quality and access between urban and rural areas, and between different socio-economic classes, also remained persistent issues.

The journey of social reformation and educational development in Pakistan has been complex and multifaceted. Despite the myriad challenges, Pakistan has made considerable strides. Over the years, literacy rates have improved, and social norms have gradually evolved. Women's participation in all walks of life has increased, though there is still a long way to go to achieve gender equality.

In retrospect, the endeavours towards social reformation and education signify Pakistan's commitment to evolving into a diverse yet united, progressive society. As the nation navigates the path to success, understanding these efforts provides crucial insights into Pakistan's resilience and the foundational building blocks of its societal structure.

Defence and Foreign Policy

In the wake of its inception, Pakistan faced several security challenges and the task of establishing an international identity.

The partition-induced communal violence had highlighted the country's vulnerability, shaping the early focus of its defence and foreign policies.

Defence Policy

From the outset, defence was a critical area of focus for Pakistan. The country's geopolitical location, the hostility with India, and the internal security issues necessitated a robust defence policy. The Partition violence and the ensuing refugee crisis underlined the urgency of a strong defence mechanism.

One of the most significant steps taken was the establishment of the Pakistan Armed Forces. Inherited were a portion of the British Indian Army, Navy, and Air Force personnel, which were restructured into Pakistan's military. However, the division of military assets between India and Pakistan was unequal, leaving the latter at a disadvantage.

The first India-Pakistan war over Kashmir in 1947-48, coming just months after independence, highlighted the necessity of a strong military. In the subsequent years, Pakistan significantly increased its defence expenditure and embarked on a drive to strengthen its military capabilities.

Pakistan also sought alliances to bolster its defence. It joined the Southeast Asia Treaty Organization (SEATO) and the Central Treaty Organization (CENTO), hoping to gain military aid and strategic support against potential threats. However, the benefits of these alliances were mixed, and Pakistan eventually withdrew from SEATO and CENTO in the early 1970s.

The development of nuclear capabilities was another critical aspect of Pakistan's defence policy. Following India's nuclear tests in 1974, Pakistan accelerated its own nuclear program. Although it attracted international criticism and sanctions, Pakistan viewed it as vital for maintaining a strategic balance in South Asia.

Foreign Policy

Pakistan's foreign policy in its early years was primarily shaped by its security concerns and the quest for international recognition. It adopted a policy of non-alignment in the Cold War but leaned towards the Western bloc due to shared security interests. The US-Pakistan alliance emerged as a significant aspect of its foreign policy, leading to substantial economic and military aid from the US. In recent years, attempts have been made to reduce Pakistan's reliance on the U.S. During Imran Khan's government, Pakistan's refusal to give military bases to America soured relations. Despite this, those in the administrative establishment of Pakistan view the U.S. as critical for Pakistan's survival. Mr. Khan was ousted months later via a vote of no confidence, days after the foreign ministry received a diplomatic cable from the U.S. government stating their desire to see Khan's ousting.

Relations with India remained strained due to unresolved issues like Kashmir. The war in 1965 and the subsequent Tashkent Agreement failed to bring lasting peace. The separation of East Pakistan in 1971, aided by India, further soured the relations.

Pakistan's relationship with China has been a cornerstone of its foreign policy. Recognizing China in 1950, Pakistan became one of the first countries to establish diplomatic relations with the People's Republic. The Sino-Pak friendship, underscored by their shared rivalry with India, has grown over the years, encompassing defence, economic, and diplomatic cooperation.

Pakistan's foreign policy also focused on building solidarity with Muslim countries. It became a founding member of the Organization of Islamic Cooperation (OIC) in 1969, aiming to promote Muslim unity and address common concerns. Pakistan was successful in organizing the Eighth Extraordinary Summit in late 2021, with a focus on America's exit from Afghanistan and the plight of the Afghan people. Just four months later,

Pakistan Foreign Minister Shah Mehmood Qureshi hosted the 48th session of the Council of Foreign Ministers of OIC. This was a special achievement of Pakistani foreign policy, showcasing its standing as a major player in the Islamic world.

In conclusion, defence and foreign policy have been critical aspects of Pakistan's journey as a new nation. The country faced numerous security challenges and navigated complex international dynamics in its early years. Despite the many trials, Pakistan made significant strides in strengthening its defence and carving out its place on the international stage. As the nation's story unfolds, it's essential to understand these aspects of its path, which have significantly influenced its present and future trajectory.

Conclusion: Triumph Amidst Trials

As we look back at the initial years of Pakistan's existence, what emerges is a picture of a fledgling nation grappling with manifold trials yet persisting on a path toward progress. The challenges confronting the nascent state were monumental - ranging from handling an unprecedented refugee crisis and establishing new political structures to rebuilding an economy from the ground up, and initiating necessary social reforms. Yet, despite the arduous journey, the resilience and determination that the nation exhibited is remarkable.

The refugee crisis at the onset of partition was an immediate test of Pakistan's strength and compassion. The trials were many - from the sheer scale of displacement to the humanitarian crisis that ensued. Yet, the country's response to this adversity was indicative of its resolve. Significant efforts were put forth to accommodate and integrate the refugees, providing them with new homes and opportunities in their new country.

In the realm of politics, the establishment of democratic institutions and the development of a constitution were significant feats. Although the path was marked by political instability, military interventions, and inter-provincial discord, the efforts towards democratic consolidation, however intermittent, signified the nation's aspiration for a democratic and inclusive polity.

The journey of economic development was laden with hurdles like a weak industrial base and limited resources. Yet, the implementation of economic plans and industrial policies, agricultural revolution, and international partnerships were pivotal in facilitating a transition from an agrarian to a semi-industrialized economy.

The nation's strides in social reformation and education are notable. Gender reforms, attempts to transform feudal norms, and the enhancement of literacy through the establishment of educational institutions, despite numerous obstacles, underscored the nation's commitment to social progress.

In the arena of defence and foreign policy, Pakistan faced and continues to face considerable challenges. The nation's geopolitical location, coupled with early hostilities, necessitated the creation of robust defence mechanisms and a dynamic foreign policy. Through strategic alliances, military strengthening, and diplomatic manoeuvring, Pakistan navigated the intricate dynamics of international relations.

While the trials were formidable, Pakistan's journey has not been devoid of triumphs. Each hurdle surmounted, each challenge met, has been a testament to the country's resilience and a step towards realizing its potential. These triumphs amidst trials should not be understated, for they provide a window into the indomitable spirit of a nation striving to establish its identity and secure its place on the world stage.

The story of Pakistan's early years is, in essence, a tale of survival, resilience, and gradual progress. While the journey is far from complete, and many trials still lay ahead, the groundwork laid in these initial years has been instrumental in shaping the nation's trajectory. As we delve further into Pakistan's path to success in the subsequent chapters, the trials and triumphs of these early years provide a valuable backdrop, setting the stage for a deeper understanding of the nation's journey.

3. POLITICAL LANDSCAPE

3.1 THE EVOLUTION OF PAKISTAN'S POLITICAL SYSTEM

Since its inception, Pakistan's political journey has been a fascinating, albeit tumultuous, saga marked by democratic aspirations, military interventions, and constitutional debates. The evolution of Pakistan's political system can be observed through distinct phases marked by a combination of constitutional development, democratic consolidation, military rule, and socio-political transformations.

Initial Years: Formation of a Democratic Framework (1947-1958)

When Pakistan was born in 1947, it was endowed with a parliamentary system of governance, inherited from British India. The new nation's political structure was further shaped by its founding leaders' vision of a democratic state that guaranteed equal rights for all its citizens.

Leading the way was the Quaid-I-Azam, Muhammad Ali Jinnah, whose articulate vision for Pakistan included a robust democratic system underpinned by constitutional governance, rule of law, and protection of minorities. As Pakistan's first Governor-General, Jinnah played a pivotal role in laying the foundations of the political system, urging the nation to uphold democratic values and principles.

However, the path to establishing a democratic framework was fraught with numerous challenges. The absence of a constitution in the initial years of independence meant that the Government of India Act of 1935, with certain modifications, served as the country's working constitution. This lack of a constitutional consensus left a void, leading to conflicts over the distribution of powers between the central and provincial governments, particularly concerning the rights of the provinces and the role of religion in the state.

The Constituent Assembly of Pakistan, formed in 1947, was tasked with drafting a constitution that would define the country's governance structure. However, the task proved challenging due to the diverse political, ethnic, and religious interests that needed to be harmonized. After nearly nine years of debate and deliberation, the Constituent Assembly finally adopted the Constitution on 23rd March 1956, officially declaring the country an Islamic Republic.

The Constitution of 1956 established a federal system with a strong centre and parliamentary form of democracy. It sought to balance the principles of parliamentary democracy with the ideological elements of Islam. The President was to be a Muslim, and the Objectives Resolution, which aimed to blend Islamic principles with democratic norms, was made a preamble to the Constitution.

While the adoption of the constitution was a significant milestone, the democratic framework continued to face considerable challenges. Issues like regional disparities, power imbalances, political instability, and the struggle between civilian and military institutions posed substantial threats. Furthermore, there was a conspicuous absence of a robust political culture, largely due to a lack of education and political awareness amongst the masses.

In conclusion, the initial years of Pakistan's political history, from 1947 to 1958, were marked by the struggle to establish a democratic framework and lay the groundwork for constitutional governance. While the process was laborious and fraught with challenges, the adoption of the constitution was a significant triumph, underscoring the nation's democratic aspirations. This period laid the foundation upon which Pakistan's political system was built, setting the stage for the ensuing political developments and transformations.

The First Military Era: Ayub Khan's Regime (1958-1969)

The political landscape of Pakistan took a dramatic turn in 1958 when General Ayub Khan, the then Commander-in-Chief of the Army, abrogated the Constitution, declared martial law, and seized power from Iskandar Mirza, Pakistan's first President. This marked the beginning of the first military regime in Pakistan, a phase that significantly transformed the political, economic, and social structure of the country.

Ayub Khan's ascension to power signified a shift from the democratic aspirations of the country's founding leaders to a military-guided political system. During his rule, Ayub Khan sought to legitimize his regime by introducing a new constitution in 1962, which replaced the parliamentary system with a presidential one. He also replaced direct elections with a system known as "Basic Democracies," composed of 80,000 elected representatives who, in turn, were eligible to vote for the President and members of the national and provincial assemblies.

The "Basic Democracies" system was presented as a fusion of traditional Pakistani culture with modern democratic norms, aimed at creating a politically conscious society from the grassroots. Critics, however, perceived it as a mechanism for Ayub Khan to consolidate his rule, as it centralized power in the hands of the President, significantly undermining democratic processes.

Despite the political changes, Ayub Khan's era, often known as the "Decade of Development," saw significant economic progress. Aided by his economic team, led by Finance Minister Muhammad Shoaib, Ayub Khan pursued a vigorous development strategy focused on industrialization and agricultural development. Policies aimed at fostering private enterprise, attracting foreign aid, and implementing Five-Year Plans resulted in a substantial increase in GNP and per capita income. The construction of major infrastructure projects, such as the Mangla and Tarbela dams, further bolstered the economy.

However, the economic development of this period was marked by growing disparities. While the western parts of the country, particularly Punjab and urban Sindh, saw significant economic growth, the eastern wing, present-day Bangladesh, and the rural populace largely remained deprived of the fruits of development. This regional and class disparity fostered resentment among marginalized groups and became a source of political unrest, leading to increased opposition towards Ayub Khan's regime.

Ayub Khan's foreign policy also shaped the course of Pakistan's political history. His alignment with the West, particularly through the US-sponsored military pacts SEATO and CENTO, marked a significant shift in Pakistan's foreign policy, triggering a relationship that has deeply influenced Pakistan's political and strategic decisions to this day.

Despite economic progress and initial popularity, Ayub Khan's regime faced increasing criticism and opposition towards the late 1960s. Critics targeted the regime's authoritarian tendencies, political repression, and the growing power of the civil-military bureaucracy. Public discontent was exacerbated by the 1965 war with India, which ended in a stalemate and was seen by many as a failure of Ayub Khan's foreign policy.

The burgeoning opposition movement led by Zulfikar Ali Bhutto, the founder of the Pakistan People's Party, and Maulana Bhashani, a popular leader from East Pakistan, fueled anti-Ayub protests across the country. The movement was further strengthened by the active participation of students, labour unions, lawyers, and journalists, marking a significant moment of political mobilization.

In conclusion, Ayub Khan's era significantly altered the political landscape of Pakistan, marking the first major military intervention in the country's politics. While his regime brought significant economic development and infrastructural advancements, it was marked by a growing democratic deficit, political repression, economic disparities, and a centralization of power. The mounting public discontent and the vigorous opposition movement towards the end of his rule underscored the intrinsic tension between military rule and the democratic aspirations of the people. This period set a precedent for the recurring cycles of military rule and democratic transition that would continue to define Pakistan's political trajectory.

Decade of Democracy and Dismemberment (1970-1977)

The 1970s ushered in a new era in Pakistan's political history, marked by democratic transition, constitutional developments, socio-economic changes, and the traumatic dismemberment of the country. This decade, under the rule of Zulfikar Ali Bhutto, saw significant political upheaval and transformation, shaping the trajectory of Pakistan's future politics.

Following General Ayub Khan's resignation in 1969, General Yahya Khan assumed the reins of power, promising to hold the first nationwide general elections on the basis of adult franchise. The elections of 1970, marking a significant democratic transition, resulted in a split mandate, with Sheikh Mujibur Rahman's Awami League securing an absolute majority in East Pakistan and Zulfikar Ali Bhutto's Pakistan People's Party (PPP) emerging as the leading party in West Pakistan.

However, the failure to transfer power to Mujibur Rahman and the subsequent military crackdown in East Pakistan led to a brutal and bloody conflict, culminating in the creation of Bangladesh in December 1971. The dismemberment of Pakistan was a profound shock, triggering a major crisis of identity and nationhood. It significantly reshaped the country's political landscape, underlining the perilous consequences of political mismanagement and the denial of democratic rights.

Post-1971, Zulfikar Ali Bhutto became the President and later the Prime Minister of a deeply wounded and divided Pakistan. Bhutto's rule was characterized by significant political changes, most notably the introduction of the 1973 Constitution. The constitution, framed with a consensus of all political parties, reestablished a parliamentary form of democracy, granting extensive rights to the provinces and incorporating Islamic provisions. It remains the supreme law of Pakistan to this day, marking a significant achievement in the country's constitutional history.

Economically, Bhutto pursued socialist policies, embarking on an extensive program of nationalization that covered industries, banks, educational institutions, and health facilities. The Bhutto era saw the pursuit of social justice as a dominant theme, with initiatives aimed at land reforms, labour rights, and empowerment of marginalized sections of society. The slogan of 'Roti, Kapda, aur Makan' (Bread, Clothing, and Shelter) became synonymous with Bhutto's commitment to uplift the poor and the downtrodden.

In terms of foreign policy, Bhutto's rule marked a departure from Pakistan's previous pro-West stance. The only other Pakistani leader to do so was Imran Khan. He pursued an active policy of non-alignment, strengthening ties with the socialist bloc and Muslim countries. His efforts led to Pakistan's increased engagement with the international community, as evidenced by the hosting of the second Organization of Islamic Countries (OIC) summit in Lahore in 1974.

However, Bhutto's rule was far from uncontroversial. While his socialist policies were popular among the masses, they drew severe criticism from industrialists, landlords, and the business community. The nationalization drive, despite its positive intent, led to economic inefficiencies, corruption, and stifled private enterprise.

Bhutto's regime was also marked by accusations of political repression. His attempts to suppress opposition, control the media, and manipulate the judiciary drew criticism and led to political instability. The 1977 elections were mired in controversy, with allegations of widespread rigging leading to a civil disobedience movement by the Pakistan National Alliance (PNA), a coalition of opposition political parties.

Bhutto's fall from power came in July 1977 when General Zia-Ul-Haq staged a military coup following months of political unrest. The military takeover brought an abrupt end to Pakistan's brief democratic interlude, marking the start of another military regime that would last for more than a decade.

In conclusion, the decade of the 1970s, marked by the Bhutto era, was a period of significant political transformation in Pakistan. While it saw the advent of democratic transition, constitutional development, and socio-economic changes, it was also marred by political instability, economic challenges, and the traumatic dismemberment of the country. The lessons from this period continue to resonate in Pakistan's political discourse, emphasizing the necessity of democratic governance, political inclusivity, and the rule of law.

The Second Military Era: Zia-ul-Haq's Regime (1977-1988)

General Zia-ul-Haq's era, from 1977 to 1988, marked the second prolonged military rule in Pakistan's history. This period had significant repercussions on Pakistan's political, social, and cultural fabric, fundamentally transforming its governance structure and state ideology.

Zia-ul-Haq seized power from Zulfikar Ali Bhutto in July 1977, justifying the coup as a necessary measure to save the country from political chaos and corruption. The coup was initially welcomed by many, given the intense political unrest following the controversial 1977 elections. However, Zia's rule soon evolved into a period of prolonged military dictatorship, characterized by widespread political repression, human rights abuses, and systematic efforts to Islamize the state and society.

The military regime under Zia was marked by a distinct shift towards a more conservative, Islamic identity for the state. This was manifested in the introduction of a series of laws and reforms under the banner of Islamization. These included the enforcement of the Hudood Ordinances, changes to the legal and judicial system, such as the introduction of Shariat courts, and the emphasis on Islamic teachings in the education system. While these measures were presented as efforts to turn Pakistan into a truly Islamic state, critics argue they led to increased sectarianism, radicalization, and a shrinking space for religious diversity.

Perhaps the most controversial and consequential event of the Zia era was the execution of former Prime Minister Zulfikar Ali Bhutto in 1979. Despite international pleas for clemency, Bhutto was hanged following a controversial trial on charges of conspiracy to commit murder. This event deepened the political divide in the country and left lasting scars on the nation's collective memory.

The Zia era also witnessed significant geopolitical events that had profound impacts on Pakistan. The Soviet invasion of Afghanistan in 1979 turned Pakistan into a frontline state in the Cold War, with Zia playing a pivotal role in orchestrating the Afghan Jihad with the support of the US and Saudi Arabia. The

Afghan War had long-lasting repercussions, leading to a massive influx of Afghan refugees, the proliferation of arms and drugs, and the rise of militancy and extremism in the region.

Economically, Zia's regime marked a departure from Bhutto's socialist policies, with a shift towards liberalization and private enterprise. This period saw an increase in remittances from Pakistanis working in the Gulf countries, following the oil boom, which helped boost the economy. However, economic growth was uneven, and wealth disparities increased. The rural-urban divide and the gap between the rich and poor intensified during this period.

Zia-ul-Haq's era ended abruptly with his death in a mysterious plane crash in August 1988. His death opened the door for a return to democracy, with general elections being held in November 1988. However, the impacts of Zia's rule continued to be felt long after his death. The shift towards Islamization, the increased role of the military in politics, the rise of religious and sectarian identities, and the repercussions of the Afghan War have significantly shaped Pakistan's political and societal trajectories in subsequent years.

In conclusion, the Zia era was a period of significant transformation for Pakistan. The impacts of Zia's policies - his Islamic reforms, his role in the Afghan War, his suppression of democratic institutions, and his economic policies - continue to resonate in Pakistan's politics, society, and culture. His regime serves as a reminder of the perils of authoritarian rule and the long-lasting impacts of geopolitical events. It underscores the importance of democratic governance, respect for human rights, and the careful management of foreign relations in shaping a nation's destiny.

Transition towards Democracy (1988-Present)

Since the end of Zia-ul-Haq's military regime in 1988, Pakistan has experienced a long and tumultuous transition towards democracy. This period has seen alternating civilian governments, two brief stints of military rule, the rise of new political actors, significant constitutional amendments, and an evolving role of the judiciary and media.

Following Zia's death, the general elections in 1988 marked the return of democracy and saw the rise of Benazir Bhutto, Zulfikar Ali Bhutto's daughter, as the first female Prime Minister in the Muslim world. Her government, however, was short-lived, dismissed by the then President Ghulam Ishaq Khan on charges of corruption in 1990, reflecting the tenuous nature of democratic governance in the early transition period.

The 1990s, often referred to as the 'decade of democracy,' was characterized by political instability, with power swinging between the Pakistan People's Party (PPP) led by Benazir Bhutto and the Pakistan Muslim League (PML-N) led by Nawaz Sharif. This period saw three democratically elected governments prematurely dismissed, frequent instances of political corruption, and escalating tensions between the civilian leadership and the military establishment.

The decade ended with the military coup in 1999, led by General Pervez Musharraf, marking another disruption in the democratic journey. Musharraf's regime (1999-2008), much like that of Zia-ul-Haq, was characterized by political repression, manipulation of constitutional structures, and an assertive foreign policy in the post-9/11 context. However, sustained domestic and international pressure led to the restoration of democracy with the general elections in 2008.

The return to democracy in 2008 heralded a new phase in Pakistan's political transition. The PPP, under the leadership of Asif Ali Zardari, Bhutto's widower, emerged victorious, marking the start of what would be the first full term of a democratically elected government in Pakistan's history. The subsequent years saw the peaceful transfer of power from one civilian government to another in 2013 and 2018, indicating a gradual consolidation of democratic norms.

This period also witnessed significant constitutional developments, most notably the 18th amendment in 2010, which reversed many of the changes made by Musharraf and earlier military rulers, reinforced parliamentary supremacy, and granted greater autonomy to the provinces.

However, widespread corruption & poor governance led to discontent of a rising educated middle class. Their discontent, growing for many years, finally found its face in Imran Khan and his Pakistan Tehreek-e-Insaf (PTI). Led by a hopeful and charged youth, the PTI saw a successful campaign in 2018 and formed the Federal government, as well as governments in four provinces.

Mr Khan inherited a large budget deficit and balance of payment crisis. Just two years into government, the COVID-19 virus disrupted the economy and brought it to a halt. In these conditions, his government imposed austerity measures to deal with these challenges. Despite having to take such measures, Mr Khan's time in government saw the economy grow at a modest pace while reducing the budget deficit and improving the balance of payments.

On the front of foreign policy, Mr. Khan faced a lot of challenges. Just six months into his government, India breached Pakistani airspace and conducted failed strikes in northern Pakistan. Still trying to acclimate to government and facing an opposition that politicized even such a breach, Imran Khan stood firm. As a result, Pakistan captured an Indian pilot. This was not just a defence victory but also helped Pakistan's foreign policy as it allowed leverage in the conflict and played a role in easing tensions.

Not all went smoothly for Imran Khan, however. The Pakistani military plays an important role in its political landscape and holds Pakistan's relationship with the U.S. dearly. Mr. Khan's efforts to reduce reliance, closer relationship with Russia & China, and refusal to give military bases to the U.S. had already irked military superiors. When Pakistan remained neutral in the Ukraine war sponsored by the U.S. government, this discontent grew among Pakistani and American establishments. Khan's time in office was, therefore, limited. In April of 2022, he was ousted from power.

After Khan, the coalition of opposition parties elected Shehbaz Sharif as the Prime Minister of Pakistan, who had anti-corruption cases against him at the time. Six months after being ousted from power, Imran Khan faced an assassination attempt while addressing a political rally. Soon enough, his supporters & party members faced intimidation tactics from the country's powerful. Not bowing down to anyone, Mr Khan was eventually arrested on May 9th. While he had to be released due to widespread protests in the country, he was arrested again months later.

Despite his popularity, Imran Khan served jail time. Out of the many cases against him, it is remarkable to note that there is not even an allegation of corruption or abuse of power from his time as Prime Minister. However, he faced the consequences of being the democratic voice of the people.

3.2 KEY POLITICAL MILESTONES AND THEIR IMPACTS

The Objectives Resolution (1949): An Ideological Foundation for Pakistan

The Objectives Resolution of 1949 is a seminal event in Pakistan's political history, providing a foundational charter for the country's constitutional and legislative journey. Drafted by

Liaquat Ali Khan, the first Prime Minister of Pakistan, it was adopted by the Constituent Assembly of Pakistan on 12th March 1949, barely two years after the nation's inception. It marked a significant attempt to merge modern democratic ideals with Islamic principles, embodying the vision of Pakistan as an Islamic democratic state.

The Objectives Resolution essentially laid out the fundamental principles that would guide the formulation of the future constitution of Pakistan. It emphasized the principles of democracy, freedom, equality, tolerance, and social justice, as enshrined in the teachings of Islam. It declared that sovereignty belongs to Allah, with the state of Pakistan merely acting as a trustee tasked to implement His will.

In addition to its democratic and Islamic principles, the Resolution also guaranteed the protection of minority rights, outlining that "adequate provision shall be made for the minorities to freely profess and practice their religions and develop their cultures." This was significant in ensuring the democratic vision of the state by emphasizing inclusivity and religious freedom.

The implications of the Objectives Resolution were far-reaching and profound, shaping the political and constitutional discourse in Pakistan. Despite ongoing debate over its interpretation, the Resolution served as a preamble to the constitutions of 1956, 1962, and 1973, marking its sustained relevance in defining the identity of the state.

However, the Objectives Resolution also sparked controversy, particularly concerning the balance between Islamic and democratic principles. Critics argue that by proclaiming sovereignty to Allah, the Resolution introduced ambiguity, allowing subsequent rulers to manipulate this clause to legitimize autocratic rule under the guise of Islamic principles. The emphasis on Islamic provisions raised concerns about the marginalization of religious minorities and the potential for religious dogma to supersede democratic norms.

Additionally, the Objectives Resolution played a crucial role in shaping Pakistan's legal framework, with the Supreme Court referring to it in various landmark judgments. It provided a blueprint for incorporating Islamic provisions into the law of the land, influencing legislation such as the Hudood Ordinances and the Blasphemy Laws.

In conclusion, the Objectives Resolution remains a cornerstone in Pakistan's political history, laying the ideological foundation of the state. It symbolizes the synthesis of Islamic principles with democratic ideals, encapsulating the unique character of Pakistan's political and constitutional journey. However, it also reflects the enduring challenges in navigating the delicate balance between religious identity and democratic governance in Pakistan, with its interpretations influencing the nation's trajectory in profound and complex ways.

The Constitution of 1956 and the Declaration of the Islamic Republic

Nearly a decade after achieving independence, Pakistan adopted its first constitution on March 23, 1956. The delay in the constitution-making reflected the country's struggle to reconcile diverse regional, ethnic, and religious interests and to establish a political consensus. Nonetheless, the Constitution of 1956 was a significant milestone in Pakistan's political journey, formally transforming the country into an 'Islamic Republic' and establishing fundamental rights and principles for governance.

The Constitution of 1956 was based on the principles outlined in the Objectives Resolution of 1949. It upheld the Islamic character of the state while ensuring democratic governance and protection of minority rights. The preamble of the constitution reiterated that sovereignty belongs to Allah, and the state of

Pakistan would exercise its powers and authority within the limits prescribed by Him.

For the first time in Pakistan's history, the constitution declared the country an 'Islamic Republic,' signifying the country's unique ideological basis, wherein Islamic principles and democratic governance were to coexist. It also provided a legal framework for the implementation of Islamic laws.

The constitution stipulated a parliamentary form of government, with the President as the ceremonial head of state and the Prime Minister as the head of government. It delineated the separation of powers among the executive, legislative, and judicial branches, intending to establish a system of checks and balances.

One of the major features of the 1956 Constitution was its emphasis on fundamental rights. These rights, detailed in Part II of the constitution, included equality of status, social, economic, and political justice, freedom of thought, expression, belief, faith, worship, and association, protection of property rights, and the right to fair trial. It also laid out the Directive Principles of State Policy, serving as guidelines for the government in making laws and policies.

However, the constitution also grappled with the contentious issue of provincial autonomy, an issue that would continue to shape Pakistan's political landscape. While it recognized the existence of two provinces, East and West Pakistan, the issue of representation and resource allocation between the two remained a point of contention.

Despite its progressive and democratic features, the Constitution of 1956 was short-lived. It was abrogated by the military coup of Ayub Khan in 1958, marking the onset of the first military regime in Pakistan. However, it set a precedent for the subsequent constitutions, providing a blueprint for the country's political system and governance structure.

In conclusion, the Constitution of 1956 was a key political milestone in Pakistan's history. It formalized the ideological character of the state, established fundamental rights, and outlined the structure for democratic governance. Despite its eventual abrogation, the Constitution of 1956 remains an important reference point in understanding the evolution of Pakistan's constitutional and political journey.

The Era of Zulfikar Ali Bhutto (1971-1977): A Time of Political Transformation and Upheaval

The era of Zulfikar Ali Bhutto, the 9th Prime Minister of Pakistan, marked a profound shift in Pakistan's political landscape. Bhutto ascended to power during one of the most tumultuous periods in the country's history, following the tragic dismemberment of East Pakistan and the emergence of Bangladesh in 1971. His rule, characterized by charismatic leadership, populist policies, and international realignments, left an indelible mark on Pakistan's political, economic, and social fabric.

Bhutto's reign is marked by several key milestones, perhaps the most significant being the creation of Pakistan's current constitution in 1973. Bhutto championed the constitution-making process, creating consensus among the country's disparate political parties, which resulted in the country's most durable constitution. The 1973 Constitution reaffirmed Pakistan's Islamic identity while establishing a parliamentary democracy, clearly defining the separation of powers and a comprehensive bill of fundamental rights.

Furthermore, Bhutto's era saw a radical shift in economic policies. Bhutto's socialist-leaning government introduced extensive nationalization measures, affecting key industries such as banking, steel, chemical, cement and cooking oil. The nationalization drive aimed to reduce income disparities and establish control over the 'commanding heights' of the economy. While the nationalization process did increase state control, it also led to a decline in industrial growth and bred inefficiencies.

Another key aspect of Bhutto's rule was the emphasis on enhancing Pakistan's international standing. Bhutto, a seasoned diplomat, reoriented Pakistan's foreign policy, strengthening ties with the Islamic world and the Non-Aligned Movement, while maintaining a balance in relations with the superpowers. This period witnessed the successful hosting of the 2nd Organisation of Islamic Conference (OIC) summit in Lahore in 1974, which boosted Pakistan's image as a leader in the Islamic world.

On the darker side, Bhutto's era also saw political polarization, marked by allegations of authoritarianism and repression. The 1977 general elections sparked widespread political unrest due to allegations of rigging, leading to the Pakistan National Alliance's (PNA) countrywide protests demanding Bhutto's resignation.

These protests marked the beginning of the end for Bhutto's regime. In a shocking turn of events, Bhutto's government was overthrown in a military coup led by his appointed Chief of Army Staff, General Zia-ul-Haq. Bhutto was later controversially tried and executed for a politically motivated murder charge, marking a tragic end to a significant era in Pakistan's history.

In conclusion, Zulfikar Ali Bhutto's era, while relatively short-lived, was a time of profound transformation for Pakistan. His charismatic leadership, populist policies, and daring international realignments made him a popular leader. However, the controversies, particularly the alleged election rigging and the subsequent military coup, underscored the fragility of democracy in Pakistan. Bhutto's era thus serves as a reflection of Pakistan's ongoing struggle between democratic aspirations and the realities of political instability.

Zia-ul-Haq's Islamization Drive and the 8th Amendment (1977-1988): Shaping a New Ideological Trajectory

Following his military coup in July 1977, General Muhammad Zia-ul-Haq embarked on an ambitious project to redefine Pakistan's national ideology through a widespread Islamization drive and major constitutional amendments. This transformative period drastically reshaped the political, social, and legal fabric of the country, with lasting implications for its future.

Zia-ul-Haq's Islamization campaign was part of a broader strategy to legitimize his military regime, which lacked a democratic mandate. By positioning himself as a champion of Islamic values, Zia hoped to gain the support of religious groups and sidestep demands for a return to democratic rule.

The Islamization drive touched virtually every aspect of Pakistani society. Zia introduced Islamic punishments (the Hudood Ordinances), established Shariat Courts, and made Islamic Studies compulsory in schools. Furthermore, he enforced observance of Islamic rituals, such as prayers and fasting, in public offices. These measures, although controversial, resonated with sections of the population, bolstering Zia's image as an Islamic leader.

Perhaps the most significant change under Zia's rule was the introduction of the 8th Amendment to the Constitution of 1973. The amendment, passed in 1985, vested sweeping powers in the President, including the right to dissolve the National Assembly and dismiss the Prime Minister. This dramatically shifted the balance of power from the Parliament to the President, altering the dynamics of Pakistan's political system.

Furthermore, the amendment introduced the concept of the "Islamic way of life" as a constitutional principle and made the

Shariat Court the final arbiter on whether laws were in accordance with Islam. This further entrenched the role of Islam in the country's legal and political framework, giving the judiciary a more prominent role in shaping public policy.

However, Zia's Islamization drive was met with strong opposition from various quarters. Critics argued that the measures were a ploy to consolidate power, undermined the rights of women and minorities, and fostered a culture of intolerance. Furthermore, the 8th Amendment was seen as a departure from democratic principles, undermining the parliament's authority and fostering a culture of political instability.

Despite the controversy, Zia's Islamization drive had a profound and lasting impact on Pakistan. It significantly altered the country's legal, social, and political landscape, embedding Islamic principles deeper into the public sphere. It also shifted the balance of power in the political system, with the legacy of the 8th Amendment continuing to shape the country's political dynamics.

In conclusion, Zia-ul-Haq's Islamization drive and the 8th Amendment marked a pivotal period in Pakistan's history. While they helped solidify Zia's rule and gave Islam a more prominent role in public life, they also stirred controversy and altered the country's political dynamics in significant ways. The legacy of this period continues to reverberate in contemporary Pakistan, shaping its ideological trajectory and political landscape.

The Lawyers' Movement and the Restoration of Judiciary (2007-2009): A Fight for Rule of Law and Democracy

The Lawyers' Movement, also known as the 'Black Coat Protests', marked a watershed moment in Pakistan's political history. Spanning from March 2007 to March 2009, this nationwide campaign led by lawyers aimed to restore independent judges dismissed by General Pervez Musharraf, highlighting the struggle for the rule of law and the restoration of democracy in the country.

The movement was sparked off when Musharraf, then President and Chief of Army Staff, suspended Chief Justice Iftikhar Chaudhry in March 2007 on charges of misconduct and misuse of authority. The move was widely seen as an attempt by Musharraf to prevent legal challenges to his plan to seek another term as president while still holding the position of army chief.

The dismissal was met with an unprecedented backlash from Pakistan's legal fraternity. Lawyers across the country took to the streets in their black suits, leading protests, and rallies, calling for the reinstatement of the dismissed judges and an independent judiciary. The protests were marked by images of lawyers clashing with police, enduring tear gas and arrests, symbolizing their determination to uphold the rule of law.

The Lawyers' Movement galvanized other sections of society as well. Political parties including Imran Khan's PTI, civil society groups, activists, and the media joined in the calls for judicial independence and an end to military rule. The protests intensified following Musharraf's imposition of a state of emergency in November 2007, which led to the dismissal of most of the judiciary, including the reinstated Chief Justice Chaudhry.

The movement culminated in a 'Long March' in March 2009, a massive protest rally from different cities towards the capital, Islamabad. The march, which saw tens of thousands of participants, demanded the immediate restoration of the dismissed judges.

The sustained pressure from the Lawyers' Movement eventually forced the government's hand. On March 16, 2009, the newly elected government announced the reinstatement of Chief Justice Chaudhry and other dismissed judges, marking a significant victory for the movement.

The Lawyers' Movement was a powerful demonstration of civil society's ability to challenge authoritarian rule and fight for democratic principles. It marked a turning point in the country's political trajectory, leading to the restoration of democracy and a stronger, more independent judiciary.

Moreover, the movement underscored the crucial role of the judiciary in upholding democratic principles and the rule of law. It brought into focus the importance of judicial independence, setting a precedent for resistance against executive overreach.

In conclusion, the Lawyers' Movement was a pivotal chapter in Pakistan's history, marked by the resilience of its legal fraternity and civil society in the face of authoritarianism. The successful restoration of the judiciary was not just a victory for the lawyers but a triumph for democratic principles, rule of law, and civil society's role in defending these values. The echoes of this movement can still be heard today, serving as a reminder of the strength of unified, peaceful resistance.

PTI's struggle for the restoration of democracy (April 2022 onwards)

After Imran Khan's ouster in April 2022, his party called for free and fair elections. Their first attempt was on the 25th of May, in the form of a march to Islamabad. They were met with police brutality and tear gas. Women and children were not spared by police officers, and images of PTI's female leadership being attacked mercilessly shook the world. Avoiding more bloodshed and chaos, Khan refused to move further towards the parliament.

Months later, Mr. Khan was marching towards Islamabad again when an assassination attempt was made on him. The attempt ended up killing a PTI supporter while injuring nine members of PTI including Mr. Khan. Days earlier, a prominent journalist from Pakistan—Arshad Sharif—was assassinated in Kenya for his pro-democracy stances.

PTI further dissolved its government in Punjab on 14 January 2023. According to Pakistan's constitution, elections should have been held by 14th April 2023. However, the government's refusal to do so marked the unofficial dissolution of the constitution. In order to revive the constitution and its application, Mr. Khan continued his struggle.

However, on 9th May, he was abducted by Pakistani law enforcement agencies from inside Islamabad High Court. His arrest led to violent protests across the country with unprecedented mob attacks on military instalments across the country. While public pressure and court norms led to a Supreme Court order to free Imran Khan, thousands of his supporters and party members were picked up and disappeared. He was later rearrested and dozens of cases were made against him. The Pakistani military marked 9th May as a black day and a massive crackdown was launched against Khan's party as a result PTI was almost dismantled.

3.3 CURRENT POLITICAL HURDLES: NAVIGATING THE COMPLEXITIES OF A DEVELOPING DEMOCRACY

Pakistan's political landscape, while showing signs of resilience and evolution, continues to grapple with various challenges. These challenges range from the consolidation of democratic institutions, corruption, social and ethnic fragmentation, to the fragile civil-military relations. Navigating these hurdles is crucial for Pakistan's political stability and its aspirations to emerge as a mature and inclusive democracy.

Consolidation of Democratic Institutions

Despite successful democratic transitions in recent years, the institutionalization of democracy in Pakistan remains an uphill task. The country's political parties often lack internal democracy, and dynastic politics remains a pervasive feature. This undermines political competition, and the emergence of new leaders stifles constructive debate on policies. The weakness of political parties hinders the development of a robust democratic culture.

The country's political institutions, including the parliament and judiciary, also face challenges. The parliament's effectiveness is often limited by political wrangling, with legislation often getting stuck in the crossfire of competing political interests. The judiciary, despite strides made during the Lawyers' Movement, continues to struggle with a massive backlog of cases, resource constraints, and accusations of overstepping its mandate.

Corruption and Accountability

Corruption remains a deeply entrenched problem, affecting political stability and undermining development efforts. While anti-corruption initiatives have gained prominence, effective accountability remains elusive. Politically motivated witch hunts and selective accountability often overshadow genuine efforts to combat corruption, eroding public trust in accountability institutions.

Social and Ethnic Fragmentation

Pakistan's diverse ethnic and social fabric, while a source of richness, also poses challenges for political cohesion. Ethnic and sectarian tensions sometimes spill over into the political arena, leading to instability and violence. The use of ethnic and sectarian identities for political mobilization can further exacerbate these tensions.

Furthermore, socio-economic disparities between different regions fuel a sense of deprivation and resentment. The perceived dominance of Punjab, the most populous province, often leads to grievances among smaller provinces. This demands a more balanced and inclusive approach to development that takes into account the unique needs and aspirations of different regions.

Civil-Military Relations

The delicate balance of civil-military relations remains a pressing challenge for Pakistan's politics. The military's dominant role in security and foreign policy, often perceived as overshadowing civilian institutions, can create tensions. While the military's role is partly a product of historical and geopolitical realities, a more equitable civil-military partnership is crucial for political stability and democratic consolidation.

Towards a More Inclusive and Robust Democracy

In conclusion, Pakistan's political hurdles are complex and deeply rooted. However, they are not insurmountable. To overcome these challenges, a concerted effort is needed to strengthen democratic institutions, enhance political competition, tackle corruption, and foster social cohesion. This includes strengthening the internal democracy of political parties, empowering parliament, and enhancing the judiciary's efficiency.

Similarly, the fight against corruption needs a more comprehensive approach, one that goes beyond high-profile prosecutions to systemic reforms. Addressing social and ethnic fragmentation requires inclusive policies that address regional disparities and promote interfaith harmony.

Finally, crafting a more balanced civil-military relationship is crucial. This involves creating space for civilian institutions in security and foreign policy decision-making and fostering a culture of mutual respect and cooperation.

In navigating these hurdles, Pakistan has an opportunity to consolidate its democracy, ensure political stability, and harness its immense potential for progress. The journey is challenging, but with resilience, introspection, and reform, a more robust and inclusive democracy is within reach.

4. ECONOMIC CHALLENGES

4.1 THE STATE OF PAKISTAN'S ECONOMY: AN OVERVIEW

Pakistan, the world's sixth most populous country, is strategically positioned at the crossroads of South Asia, Central Asia, and the Middle East. This advantageous location, coupled with a wealth of natural resources and a vibrant population, offers significant potential for economic growth and development. However, the economic trajectory of Pakistan has been marked by periods of growth and significant challenges, making it a complex landscape to navigate.

Economic Structure and Performance: Charting Pakistan's Economic Journey

Pakistan's economy is a complex blend of traditional and modern sectors, shaped by its unique geography, historical events, and evolving policy choices. Its economic structure, characterized by the sectors of agriculture, industry, and services, reflects this complex interplay.

Agricultural Backbone and Emerging Services

Traditionally, Pakistan's economy has been heavily reliant on agriculture. With the country's fertile soil and a climate suitable for various crops, the agricultural sector has been a cornerstone of the economy. Despite a decline in its overall contribution to GDP, the sector still employs nearly 40% of Pakistan's workforce and forms the backbone of rural livelihoods. It supplies critical raw materials to the industrial sector, especially the textile industry, Pakistan's largest industry and the primary source of its export earnings.

However, the economic landscape has been gradually shifting, with the services sector emerging as the most significant contributor to Pakistan's GDP. This sector, encompassing areas like telecommunications, finance, retail, and public services, has been on the rise due to several factors. Economic liberalization policies, growth in consumer demand, and advancements in technology have propelled the services sector's growth. The burgeoning middle class, combined with increasing urbanization, has fueled demand for a variety of services, from retail and entertainment to education and healthcare.

Industrial Challenges

While the industrial sector plays a crucial role in the economy, providing employment, contributing to GDP, and driving exports, it has faced several challenges. Power shortages and energy crises have been significant obstacles, disrupting industrial production and hampering growth. Infrastructure bottlenecks, including inadequate transport and logistics facilities, have also posed challenges. Additionally, issues like low productivity, limited technological advancement, and regulatory constraints have restrained the industrial sector's potential.

Economic Performance: A Mixed Picture

Pakistan's economic performance presents a mixed picture. The economy has shown resilience, with periods of decent growth rates, particularly in the 2000s, when GDP growth averaged around 5%. The country has also made progress in reducing poverty and improving human development indicators.

However, the economic journey has not been smooth, with frequent episodes of macroeconomic instability interrupting growth. High fiscal and current account deficits, coupled with high inflation rates, have been recurring problems. These challenges have often necessitated economic stabilization programs with the International Monetary Fund (IMF), providing temporary relief but also bringing stringent policy conditions.

In Conclusion

Pakistan's economic structure and performance provide insights into the country's economic journey. The transition from an agrarian economy to a more diversified one, the challenges facing the industrial sector, and the mixed economic performance reflect the complexities of managing an economy in a challenging socio-political and global environment. Looking forward, the task for Pakistan's policymakers is to manage these complexities effectively, fostering an environment conducive to sustainable and inclusive growth.

Challenges and Opportunities: Pakistan's Economic Landscape

Pakistan's economy, while rich in potential, faces significant hurdles. These challenges are multifaceted, ranging from fiscal deficits to structural issues and human capital development. However, alongside these challenges lie immense opportunities that, if tapped into effectively, could set the country on a path to substantial economic progress.

Economic Challenges

One of the most critical economic challenges that Pakistan faces is its fiscal situation. Pakistan has one of the lowest tax-to-GDP ratios globally, attributable to a narrow tax base, rampant tax evasion, and administrative inefficiencies in tax collection. This paucity of revenues, coupled with high expenditures, primarily driven by debt servicing and defence spending, result in sizable fiscal deficits. These deficits then necessitate heavy borrowing, leading to a mounting public debt burden.

Another significant challenge is energy. Power shortages and energy crises have frequently disrupted the country's economic activity, affecting both industry and households. Despite efforts to diversify energy sources and increase power generation capacity, the energy issue remains a substantial drag on Pakistan's economic potential.

Structural issues within the economy also pose significant challenges. These include a low savings and investment rate, limiting the funds available for productive investments. Additionally, despite improvements in education and health outcomes over the years, the quality of human capital remains a challenge due to issues with the quality of education, skills mismatch in the labour market, and uneven health outcomes.

Economic Opportunities

Despite these formidable challenges, there are also significant opportunities that Pakistan can leverage. A major one is the China-Pakistan Economic Corridor (CPEC), part of China's Belt and Road Initiative. This ambitious project promises to boost Pakistan's economy by enhancing infrastructure, improving energy supply, and facilitating regional connectivity. However, it also necessitates careful management to prevent unsustainable debt burdens and protect social and environmental outcomes.

Another critical opportunity is Pakistan's demographic structure. Pakistan has a youthful population, which can provide a significant demographic dividend. If harnessed effectively through investments in education and skills development, this young workforce can drive economic growth and innovation.

The expansion of digital technology also offers significant opportunities. By harnessing the power of digital technologies, Pakistan can boost economic productivity, enhance service delivery, and create new avenues for entrepreneurship and job creation. Digital finance, e-commerce, and online education are areas that hold substantial potential for growth.

Conclusion

Pakistan's economy presents a unique mix of challenges and opportunities. These challenges are daunting, yet not insurmountable. The opportunities are promising yet require effective strategies to be realized fully. Tackling the challenges and harnessing the opportunities necessitates a comprehensive and long-term approach, focused on structural reforms, investment in human capital, and policies that foster innovation and inclusiveness. With the right approach, Pakistan can transform these challenges into opportunities, charting a path toward a more prosperous and resilient economy.

Policy Interventions and Economic Reforms: Crafting Pakistan's Economic Future

Pakistan's economic challenges and opportunities necessitate effective policy interventions and economic reforms. These reforms must span various economic sectors, from fiscal and monetary policies to structural reforms in energy, industry, education, and beyond. These policy measures must be backed by a robust institutional framework and an enabling political environment to ensure their effective implementation.

Fiscal and Monetary Reforms

Fiscal reforms are a critical need for Pakistan. They should aim at enhancing revenue generation and optimizing expenditures. Reforming the tax system to broaden the tax base, simplify tax structures, and improve tax administration can help increase tax revenues. Similarly, expenditure reforms should focus on improving public sector efficiency, prioritizing development spending, and reducing non-productive expenditures.

Monetary policy reforms also hold substantial importance. Pakistan's central bank, the State Bank of Pakistan, should continue to strive for price stability while also fostering financial sector development. Regulatory reforms to enhance the banking sector's efficiency and inclusivity, alongside measures to develop the capital market, can help mobilize savings and channel them into productive investments.

Energy and Industrial Reforms

Energy sector reforms are crucial to addressing Pakistan's energy issues. These reforms should aim at diversifying energy sources, promoting renewable energy, improving energy efficiency, and reforming energy pricing and subsidies. The objective should be to ensure a sustainable, affordable, and reliable energy supply to support economic activity.

Industrial reforms should focus on improving the business environment and fostering innovation. Policies to ease doing business, enhance access to finance for SMEs, promote skill development, and foster research and innovation can help boost industrial productivity and competitiveness.

Human Capital Development

Human capital development is another key area requiring policy attention. Reforms in education should focus on enhancing the quality of education, promoting skill-based learning, and reducing disparities in educational outcomes. Similarly, health sector reforms should aim at improving health services' accessibility and quality, particularly for the underprivileged sections of society.

Conclusion: The Road Ahead

Pakistan's economic challenges are indeed formidable, yet they are not insurmountable. With effective policy interventions and economic reforms, the country can overcome these challenges and harness its immense economic potential. These reforms will not yield results overnight; they require a long-term commitment, political will, and persistence. Yet, the rewards - a more prosperous, resilient, and inclusive economy - are worth the effort. As the country embarks on this reform journey, the goal should be to ensure that the benefits of economic progress are widely shared, leading to improved living standards for all Pakistanis.

4.2 KEY ECONOMIC HURDLES AND THEIR ROOTS

Fiscal Deficit and High Debt Levels

Pakistan's economy has long been under the strain of a substantial fiscal deficit and mounting public debt, imposing severe limitations on its growth and development capabilities. The fiscal deficit, driven by a combination of low revenues and high public expenditures, is a primary concern.

The revenue generation capacity of Pakistan is among the weakest in the world, contributing to the persistent budgetary deficit. On the expenditure side, Pakistan's public spending is concentrated on defence and debt servicing, leaving scarce resources for development and social sector spending. This fiscal imbalance prompts a continual cycle of borrowing, increasing the country's public debt to alarming levels.

The high debt levels also mean a significant proportion of government resources are allocated towards debt servicing, further squeezing the space for development spending. Over time, this borrowing has led to a snowballing of public debt, locking the country into a vicious cycle of borrowing, high-interest payments, and more borrowing.

The consequences are multi-dimensional, creating an environment of macroeconomic instability and reducing the state's capacity to finance development projects and provide public services, thus negatively impacting the overall economy.

Low Tax-to-GDP Ratio

One of the critical structural challenges for Pakistan's economy is the chronically low tax-to-GDP ratio, one of the lowest globally. This situation has several roots, including a narrow tax base, widespread tax evasion, and administrative inefficiencies in tax collection.

The narrow tax base is due to numerous exemptions and concessions, a lack of progressivity in tax rates, and a significant informal sector, which remains largely outside the tax net. Tax evasion is rampant and perpetuated by weak enforcement, corruption, and a lack of taxpayer trust in the government's use of funds.

These issues are exacerbated by inefficiencies in tax administration, including cumbersome procedures, lack of automation, and weak auditing capacities. The low tax-to-GDP ratio leads to inadequate public revenues, limiting the government's ability to invest in development and social services and causing higher fiscal deficits.

Energy Crisis

Pakistan's economic performance is severely hindered by its long-standing energy crisis. This crisis, characterized by frequent power outages and gas shortages, is a significant barrier to industrial productivity and economic growth.

The roots of the energy crisis are manifold. They include a heavy reliance on imported fuels, inefficient energy infrastructure, energy theft, and a lack of investment in renewable and indigenous energy sources. The mispricing of energy and large-scale energy subsidies have also led to fiscal challenges and discouraged energy conservation and efficiency.

This energy crisis affects all economic sectors, disrupting industrial production, deterring foreign and local investment, and adding to the hardships of consumers. The energy crisis is a multi-dimensional issue, reflecting structural, governance, and financial challenges that need to be addressed comprehensively.

Unemployment and Low Human Capital

Unemployment, underemployment, and a lack of skilled human capital are other significant challenges facing Pakistan's economy. Despite a young and growing labour force, Pakistan has struggled to create sufficient quality jobs to absorb new entrants and reduce unemployment.

Low human capital development further compounds this challenge. Despite improvements in educational access, issues with the quality of education, skill mismatches, and disparities in educational outcomes persist. These factors limit the ability of Pakistan's labour force to contribute effectively to economic growth.

Moreover, labour market dynamics and structural factors, such as low female labour force participation and high informality, add to these challenges. The issues of unemployment and low human capital are, therefore, intricately linked and reflect deeper socio-economic and structural challenges in Pakistan's economy.

Roots of Economic Hurdles

To understand the roots of Pakistan's economic hurdles, one must delve into the interplay of historical, political, institutional, and socio-economic factors that have shaped the country's economic trajectory.

Historical Roots

Historically, the partition from India left Pakistan with a skewed economic structure. It inherited a narrow industrial and taxation base, and an agrarian economy with significant feudal influences. These historical imbalances have persisted, impacting the evolution of the country's economic institutions and policies.

Political Factors

Politically, Pakistan's frequent shifts between civilian and military rule have affected policy continuity and long-term planning. Short political cycles often prioritize short-term gains over long-term development needs, leading to inconsistent policymaking and implementation. This lack of political stability and policy continuity has hindered the development of a strong economic structure.

Institutional Weaknesses

Institutional weaknesses also contribute significantly to Pakistan's economic challenges. Weak governance, corruption, lack of transparency, and inadequate regulatory enforcement undermine economic performance and deter investment. Moreover, institutional deficiencies in tax administration contribute to the low tax-to-GDP ratio, while weak regulatory and policy frameworks impede the resolution of the energy crisis.

Socio-Economic Factors

Socio-economic factors, including high population growth, inequality, and low human capital development, also play a critical role. High population growth puts pressure on the government to provide public services and create jobs for a rapidly growing labour force. Socio-economic inequality, stemming from an unequal distribution of resources and opportunities, exacerbates the fiscal deficit and hampers poverty reduction efforts. Meanwhile, low human capital development, reflected in low educational attainment and skill levels, reduces labour productivity and economic competitiveness.

Geopolitical and Security Issues

Lastly, Pakistan's geopolitical location and ongoing security issues also impact its economic performance. Geopolitical tensions and security concerns deter foreign investment, affect trade relationships, and necessitate high defence spending, straining public finances.

In conclusion, the roots of Pakistan's economic hurdles are deep-seated and intertwined, reflecting the interplay of various historical, political, institutional, and socio-economic factors. Addressing these challenges, therefore, requires a comprehensive, multi-faceted approach that acknowledges and addresses these underlying factors.

Conclusion

In essence, the economic hurdles faced by Pakistan are complex, multi-dimensional, and deeply rooted in the country's historical, political, and socio-economic context. The substantial fiscal deficit and high debt levels reflect the structural imbalances in the economy, marked by low revenues and high public expenditures. The low tax-to-GDP ratio, fueled by a narrow tax base, tax evasion, and administrative inefficiencies, further exacerbates fiscal challenges.

The persistent energy crisis, characterized by frequent power outages and fuel shortages, not only hampers economic productivity but also symbolizes the broader governance and infrastructure deficiencies. Meanwhile, the issues of unemployment and low human capital development reveal the significant socio-economic challenges and structural transformations needed to tap into the potential of Pakistan's young and growing labour force.

These economic hurdles are not isolated but are interrelated, reflecting the interplay of various underlying factors. Therefore, overcoming these challenges requires comprehensive, consistent, and long-term policy measures. As we transition into the next chapter, we will explore potential solutions and strategies to address these hurdles, with an emphasis on reformative and sustainable policy interventions that can drive Pakistan's economy towards a path of robust and inclusive growth.

4.3 THE IMPACT OF GLOBALIZATION ON PAKISTAN'S ECONOMY

Globalization is a multifaceted phenomenon that has transformed the world into a closely-knit, interconnected global village. It signifies the increase in international trade, the rise of multinational corporations, the flow of capital across borders, and the intermingling of cultures. It entails not just the economic integration of countries, but also the exchange of ideas, information, and innovation.

The advent of globalization has been marked by a significant shift in the global economic landscape. With technology advancements facilitating seamless communication and transportation, the global economy has become more intertwined than ever. Countries are no longer economic islands, but participants in a complex web of global economic relationships. Each nation's economic fortunes are not just shaped by their domestic policies, but also by global economic trends, policies, and events.

In this context, the impacts of globalization on developing economies like Pakistan are profound and multifaceted. Pakistan, a country with a strategic geopolitical location and a population of over 220 million, offers an interesting case study to understand the dynamics of globalization. The aim of this chapter is to delve into how globalization has shaped Pakistan's economy – its trade, industry, labour market, technology landscape, and overall economic performance. Through this exploration, we aim to comprehend both the opportunities seized and the challenges faced by Pakistan in the era of globalization.

Overview of Pakistan's Global Economic Engagement

Pakistan, despite its challenges, has been actively participating in the global economy, showcasing a consistent effort to foster global trade relationships, encourage foreign investment, and stimulate economic development.

Pakistan's global economic integration is prominently observed in its trade relationships. The country is a member of the World Trade Organization (WTO) and has been striving to align its trade policies with global norms. It has developed a diverse trading portfolio with partners like China, the United States, and the Gulf Cooperation Council (GCC) countries, primarily exporting textiles, rice, and leather goods, and importing machinery, petroleum products, and chemicals. However, despite these efforts, Pakistan's trade deficit has been persistent due to its dependency on imported goods for its industrial and consumer sectors.

Foreign Direct Investment (FDI) has played a crucial role in Pakistan's economy, providing much-needed capital, technology, and management expertise. China, in particular, has become a significant source of FDI, largely driven by the China-Pakistan Economic Corridor (CPEC) initiative. However, FDI inflows have fluctuated over the years, affected by domestic economic conditions and global economic trends.

Remittances from overseas Pakistanis are another vital component of Pakistan's global economic engagement. These inflows have been a stable source of foreign exchange, contributing to the economy's resilience against external shocks. They have helped in poverty alleviation, improved living standards, and have supplemented the country's foreign exchange reserves.

Pakistan has also been a long-standing member of the International Monetary Fund (IMF) and the World Bank, and it has regularly engaged with these institutions for financial support and policy advice. However, this relationship has also entailed stringent reform programs and policy conditionalities aimed at fiscal consolidation and structural reforms.

Furthermore, Pakistan's engagement with global financial markets has been marked by its issuance of Eurobonds and sukuk bonds to raise foreign capital. However, the country's ability to access these markets is contingent upon its credit ratings, which are influenced by its economic performance and political stability.

In summary, Pakistan's global economic engagement is characterized by its active participation in international trade, significant reliance on remittances and FDI, engagement with international economic organizations, and interaction with global financial markets. However, this engagement also exposes Pakistan to global economic fluctuations and demands a careful balancing act to harness the benefits while managing the risks of global economic integration.

Positive Impacts of Globalization

Globalization has brought about numerous opportunities for Pakistan's economy. A significant advantage has been the access to larger markets for Pakistani products. Being part of the global trade system, Pakistan has been able to export its goods, particularly textiles, to various countries around the globe. The textile industry, which contributes significantly to Pakistan's GDP and is a major source of employment, has greatly benefited from global market access. This has provided an impetus for the growth of this sector and contributed to national income.

Globalization has also led to increased Foreign Direct Investment (FDI). Investments, notably from China under the China-Pakistan Economic Corridor (CPEC) initiative, have been pivotal in fostering economic growth and development.

FDI has not only brought in much-needed capital but has also facilitated technology transfer, aiding the enhancement of Pakistan's industrial base and technological capabilities. The infrastructure projects under CPEC, such as power plants, highways, and ports, have boosted the country's infrastructure and helped stimulate economic activities.

Another positive impact has been the improvement in human capital. Exposure to global standards and practices has led to the enhancement of skills and competencies of the Pakistani workforce. Many Pakistani professionals working for multinational corporations or overseas have been able to acquire new skills and experiences, contributing to the country's human capital development.

The diversification of Pakistan's economy is another benefit attributable to globalization. With the opening up of the economy, various sectors such as telecommunications, information technology, and services have witnessed growth and expansion. This has led to job creation and increased economic resilience by reducing dependency on a few sectors.

Access to international aid and loans has been another advantage. Engagement with international financial institutions like the IMF and the World Bank has allowed Pakistan to access financial resources necessary for economic stabilization and development projects. While these loans come with conditions, they have often helped Pakistan manage economic crises and undertake essential structural reforms.

Finally, the impact of globalization on remittances cannot be overlooked. The liberalization of global labour markets has allowed millions of Pakistanis to work abroad, particularly in the Gulf countries. These overseas Pakistanis have been regularly sending money back home, which has significantly helped in supporting the country's balance of payments and contributed to poverty reduction and improved living standards.

In conclusion, while globalization presents challenges, it also provides substantial opportunities for economic development. For Pakistan, it has opened up avenues for market access, foreign investments, technology transfers, human capital development, economic diversification, and financial support. The challenge lies in effectively leveraging these opportunities to foster sustained and inclusive economic growth.

Negative Impacts of Globalization

While globalization has brought several benefits to Pakistan, it has also exposed the country to various risks and challenges. One of the major concerns is the increased vulnerability to global economic crises. Being integrated into the global economic system, Pakistan's economy is affected by economic downturns, fluctuations in global commodity prices, and shifts in global financial markets. For instance, the global financial crisis of 2008 and the subsequent economic slowdown had a significant impact on Pakistan's economy, affecting exports, foreign investments, and remittances.

Another downside of globalization is the growing dependency on foreign aid and external debt. Pakistan has frequently relied on the International Monetary Fund (IMF) and other international lenders to manage its fiscal and balance of payments crises. However, these loans come with stringent conditions, including structural adjustment programs that often entail tough austerity measures. This dependency has also led to a significant accumulation of external debt, which imposes a heavy burden on the economy.

Globalization has also led to economic instability due to volatile capital flows. While foreign investments are crucial for economic development, they can also be very volatile, subject to global economic conditions and investor sentiments. Sudden reversals of these flows, as witnessed during periods of global financial uncertainty, can lead to financial crises.

Additionally, globalization can lead to job losses in certain sectors due to international competition. With the lowering of trade barriers, cheaper imports can outcompete local industries that are unable to match in terms of price or quality. This has been observed in Pakistan's manufacturing sector, where several industries have faced challenges due to cheaper Chinese imports.

Globalization can also exacerbate economic inequality. While some sectors and regions may flourish due to global economic integration, others may lag behind, leading to widening income and regional disparities. In Pakistan, the benefits of globalization have not been evenly distributed, contributing to inequality.

Lastly, environmental degradation is a significant concern. Rapid industrialization and economic development, often pursued without adequate environmental safeguards, can lead to environmental degradation. In Pakistan, issues such as air and water pollution, deforestation, and climate change are pressing concerns. The country ranks high on the global climate risk index, indicating its vulnerability to climate change—a problem significantly influenced by global patterns of production and consumption.

In summary, while globalization provides opportunities for economic growth and development, it also brings significant risks and challenges. For Pakistan, managing these challenges requires effective economic management, careful policymaking, and a balanced approach that harnesses the benefits of globalization while minimizing its adverse impacts.

Policy Responses and Strategies for Maximizing Benefits from Globalization

Pakistan's economic policies have sought to harness the opportunities presented by globalization while mitigating its challenges. A key part of this approach has been the pursuit of economic diversification to reduce the economy's vulnerability to external shocks. This includes promoting sectors such as information technology and telecommunications, which have the potential to penetrate global markets and create new sources of growth and employment.

Enhancing competitiveness is another important strategy. Policies have been implemented to improve the ease of doing business, upgrade infrastructure, and invest in education and skills development. The aim is to create an enabling environment where businesses can thrive and compete globally. Efforts have also been made to attract more foreign investment, particularly in areas such as manufacturing and services, to stimulate economic growth and facilitate technology transfer.

Strengthening the regulatory environment has been another focus area. This involves improving governance, enhancing transparency, and strengthening the regulatory framework to ensure a level playing field for all businesses, protect consumers, and mitigate economic risks.

Promoting sustainable practices is crucial, given the environmental challenges associated with globalization. Pakistan has been increasingly focusing on green growth strategies, aiming to pursue economic development that is environmentally sustainable. This includes promoting renewable energy, implementing environmental regulations, and investing in climate change adaptation and mitigation.

Lastly, building a resilient economy is key to navigating the uncertainties of globalization. This involves implementing sound fiscal and monetary policies, maintaining macroeconomic stability, and strengthening the country's financial system. It also requires social safety nets to protect the most vulnerable sections of society from potential adverse impacts of globalization.

In conclusion, maximizing the benefits of globalization is a complex task that requires a multi-faceted approach. By implementing these strategies, Pakistan can hope to navigate the global economic landscape effectively, seizing the opportunities it presents while tackling its inherent challenges.

Conclusion

Globalization presents a mixed bag of opportunities and challenges for Pakistan's economy. While it opens up new avenues for trade, investment, and growth, it also exposes the nation to global economic volatility, increasing inequality, and environmental challenges. Addressing these concerns calls for astute economic management, underpinned by policies geared towards economic diversification, improved competitiveness, robust regulation, sustainable practices, and social protection. Pakistan's journey in the era of globalization is a testament to its resilience and adaptability. It underscores the need for a nuanced understanding of globalization's impacts and strategic policy responses to navigate the complexities of the global economy effectively.

5. SOCIOCULTURAL FACTORS

5.1 THE ROLE OF CULTURE AND SOCIETY IN SHAPING PAKISTAN

Introduction

The intricate tapestry of Pakistan's national identity is woven with threads of diverse cultural heritage and societal norms, each of which has played a pivotal role in shaping the country's evolution. From the bustling cosmopolitan centers of Karachi and Lahore to the remote tribal regions of Khyber Pakhtunkhwa and Balochistan, Pakistan's society and culture are a testament to its rich history, profound religious influences, and vibrant ethnic mosaic. This chapter aims to delve into these multifaceted aspects of Pakistani society, exploring their impacts on the nation's development and the trajectory it continues to follow.

We will dissect the integral role of the cultural backdrop, marked by a deep-rooted historical legacy, an amalgamation of diverse ethnic influences, and a resilient Islamic identity, in defining the societal norms and structures. Moreover, we will probe how geographical diversity has shaped the lifestyles and economic activities across the region. The chapter will also provide a lens into the influence of social structures, reflecting on how they dictate social relations and economic opportunities.

Through this exploration, we will uncover how the interplay between culture and society is deeply ingrained in Pakistan's story, influencing every realm from politics to economics, from social norms to future aspirations. As we navigate this journey, we will gain a nuanced understanding of how the past continues to resonate in Pakistan's present and mould its future.

The Tapestry of Pakistani Culture

The culture of Pakistan is a richly woven tapestry, marked by the imprint of numerous civilizations, ethnic groups, and historical eras. Its roots extend deep into the annals of history, starting from one of the world's earliest urban civilizations, the Indus Valley Civilization. The advanced city planning, sophisticated artistry, and complex societal structures of this civilization laid the foundation for the region's cultural journey.

Over time, the land that is now Pakistan became a vibrant cultural crossroads, absorbing influences from Persia, Arabia, and Central Asia. Persian influences are evident in the architectural grandeur of Pakistan's historical sites, as well as in the nation's literature and poetry, most notably in the works of Allama Iqbal, Pakistan's national poet. Arabian influences significantly shaped the religious and societal fabric of the region, with the advent of Islam playing a central role in defining cultural and moral norms.

The Central Asian Turkic invasions introduced a fusion of Turkic cultural elements into the local heritage. The Mughal Empire, one of the offshoots of these invasions, left an indelible mark on the region, from the awe-inspiring architecture of Lahore's Badshahi Mosque and the Shalimar Gardens to the rich traditions of miniature painting and music.

British colonial rule added another layer to this cultural mosaic. Despite the adverse aspects of colonization, the period also ushered in modern education, legal institutions, infrastructure, and English language – elements that continue to shape contemporary Pakistani society.

The cultural landscape of Pakistan is further enriched by its diverse ethnic groups, each contributing its unique flavour to the national identity. Punjabis, Sindhis, Pashtuns, Baloch, and

Mohajirs each have their languages, literature, music, dance, and customs, adding to the colourful cultural medley.

Punjabi folk traditions, Sindhi Sufi poetry, Pashtun attan dance, Balochi embroidery, and the Urdu literature enriched by Mohajirs create a vibrant cultural matrix that defines Pakistan. This cultural diversity is also reflected in Pakistan's language landscape, with Urdu as the national language, English as the official language, and several regional languages spoken across the country.

In essence, Pakistani culture is a living testament to its history, presenting a vibrant mosaic of diverse influences, traditions, and ethnicities. This cultural heritage, complex yet cohesive, continues to shape the national identity and societal dynamics of Pakistan.

The Role of Islam

The Islamic faith is a fundamental cornerstone of Pakistan's identity. As the country formed with the primary goal of creating a separate homeland for South Asia's Muslims, Islam has always been at the heart of its national ethos. It permeates every facet of Pakistani life, shaping social norms, laws, education, and politics.

The influence of Islam is evident in Pakistan's social norms and customs. Islamic teachings dictate various aspects of personal and social conduct, shaping behaviours, attitudes, and values. Family is a core social institution in Pakistan, and the relations between family members are deeply influenced by Islamic ethics. Respect for elders, mutual responsibility among family members, hospitality, and charitable giving are some examples of Islamic virtues that are integral to Pakistani society.

Moreover, Islamic festivals such as Eid-ul-Fitr, Eid-ul-Adha, and Ramadan hold immense social and cultural significance, serving as significant events for communal bonding, festivity, and reflection. In everyday life, practices such as prayer five times a day, fasting during Ramadan, and the wearing of the hijab by many women reflect the profound imprint of Islam.

In the realm of law, the Constitution of Pakistan recognizes Islam as the state religion and asserts that all laws must be in consonance with the Quran and Sunnah. The legal system of Pakistan combines elements of civil law inherited from British and Islamic law. The Islamic Ideological Council and Federal Shariat Court are mandated to ensure the Islamic nature of legislation and legal practices.

Education in Pakistan also bears the mark of Islamic influence. Besides secular education, the religious education system, consisting of madrassas, is a prevalent parallel system, focusing on Islamic teachings, Arabic language, and religious jurisprudence. Even in the mainstream curriculum, Islamic studies are a mandatory component, aimed at imparting moral values and religious knowledge to students.

In the sphere of politics, several political parties in Pakistan have a clear Islamic orientation, advocating for laws and policies based on Islamic principles. Islam also informs the country's foreign policy, as Pakistan strives to position itself as a leader in the Muslim world.

In essence, Islam is not merely a religion in Pakistan; it is a way of life and a lens through which the country's societal, legal, educational, and political landscapes are framed. The profound influence of Islam has been instrumental in shaping the contours of Pakistan's unique identity and continues to guide its societal evolution.

Impact of Geographical Diversity

Pakistan is a country of remarkable geographical diversity, with terrains ranging from high mountain ranges and plateaus to rich agricultural plains and a coastal belt. This diversity significantly influences the country's cultural practices, lifestyles, and economic activities, resulting in a distinctive fusion of diverse regional cultures, each with its unique customs, traditions, and ways of life.

The northern regions of Pakistan are dominated by towering mountains, including some of the highest peaks in the world, such as K2 and Nanga Parbat. These regions, including Gilgit-Baltistan and Khyber Pakhtunkhwa, are home to various ethnic groups like the Pashtuns, Tajiks, and others, each with their distinct languages and traditions. The harsh mountainous environment has shaped their lifestyle, with practices revolving around pastoralism and terrace farming, supplemented by small-scale handicrafts. Their music and folk stories often reflect themes of resilience, community, and nature, underpinning the interconnection between their culture, their geography, and their livelihoods.

The Punjab and Sindh provinces, characterized by fertile plains and the expansive Indus River system, are predominantly agricultural. The Punjabi and Sindhi cultures are deeply rooted in this agrarian way of life. Cultural practices such as festivals centered around harvests, folk songs extolling rural life, and the prominence of traditional agricultural tools and techniques, all highlight the influence of geography on culture. The Punjabi Bhangra and Sindhi Ajrak, for instance, symbolize the joy of harvest and the respect for the laborious rural life.

Pakistan's coastal belt along the Arabian Sea, including the bustling city of Karachi, presents another layer of cultural complexity. The coastal communities have a distinct culture linked to the sea, with fishing being a primary occupation. The coast's strategic location has also made it a hub of trade and commerce, leading to a cosmopolitan culture marked by diversity and dynamism.

The geographical diversity extends beyond just cultural

differences; it also determines economic activities. The north, with its breathtaking mountainous landscapes, is the hub of tourism, while the fertile plains of Punjab and Sindh contribute significantly to the country's agricultural output. The coastal regions are central to the fishing industry and international trade.

In conclusion, Pakistan's geographical diversity, a blend of mountains, plains, and coastlines, has greatly influenced its cultural mosaic and economic landscape. This interplay between geography, culture, and economy underpins Pakistan's regional diversity, enriching the nation's collective identity and contributing to its unique socio-economic fabric.

The Influence of Social Structures

Social structures in Pakistan play a crucial role in shaping its society, influencing social relationships, power dynamics, and economic opportunities. The complexities of these social structures have roots in historical, cultural, and religious contexts, making their impact pervasive and often challenging to address.

One significant social structure is the caste system, a legacy of the region's Hindu past, and its influence is still apparent, particularly in rural areas. Although Islam theoretically abolished caste hierarchies, a form of it persists, with people often identified and segregated based on their ancestral occupational caste. This system influences social relationships, as it often determines marriage alliances and social interactions, thereby reinforcing social stratification. The lower castes often face social exclusion and limited economic opportunities, leading to cycles of poverty and marginalization.

Tribal affiliations, particularly evident in the northwestern provinces like Khyber Pakhtunkhwa and the semi-autonomous tribal regions, represent another influential social structure. In these areas, the tribal code of conduct, or 'Pashtunwali', governs social relations and conflict resolutions. This traditional system often holds sway over national laws, shaping power dynamics and influencing social norms. While it fosters community solidarity, it can also limit social change and perpetuate practices seen as restrictive by modern human rights standards, such as the denial of women's rights.

Family-based networks or 'biradari' systems are another societal structure that wields considerable influence, especially in political and economic spheres. These extended family networks often control power and resources, and their endorsement can significantly impact an individual's social status, political success, and economic opportunities. Patronage, nepotism, and preferential treatment within these networks can limit social mobility and foster corruption, affecting the overall functioning of society.

The influence of these social structures is profound, affecting individual life chances and societal power dynamics. They determine access to resources and opportunities, shape social norms, and often influence state policies and practices. The intersection of these structures with gender, class, and religion further compounds the social inequalities.

However, it's also crucial to note that these structures are not static; they are subject to change and evolution. There are growing challenges to these structures from within society, especially by younger generations and marginalized groups seeking social justice and equality. Understanding these social structures is vital not just for grasping Pakistan's social fabric but also for addressing the deep-seated inequalities they often engender. As Pakistan moves forward, the transformation of these structures will play a significant role in shaping its future.

Contemporary Cultural and Social Dynamics

The societal landscape of Pakistan is in a state of continuous evolution, shaped by numerous influences such as urbanization, media, women's empowerment, and the demographic shift towards a younger population.

Urbanization has been a powerful catalyst for change. As cities grow and rural populations migrate for better opportunities, there has been a significant shift in societal norms and lifestyles. City life has encouraged the growth of a more individualistic culture, contrasting with the traditional collective rural life.

The media, with its expanding reach thanks to the internet and satellite television, has also influenced society by introducing global perspectives and challenging traditional norms. The impact is especially profound among the younger generation who have access to a world of ideas, facilitating a discourse on a range of social issues from democracy to women's rights.

Indeed, women's empowerment in Pakistan has become a central issue. There has been a slow yet noticeable change in women's roles with more women participating in the workforce, politics, and public life, defying the constraints of a traditionally patriarchal society.

Finally, the youth bulge in Pakistan's demographic is creating a dynamic social force. Young people, influenced by global trends and aspiring for change, are increasingly voicing their opinions, driving societal transformation.

However, these shifts have also sparked tensions between modernity and tradition, progress and preservation. The societal and cultural dynamics of Pakistan are currently a fascinating blend of the old and the new, constantly negotiating spaces for change while maintaining a connection with their roots.

Conclusion

In conclusion, the interplay of diverse cultural influences, the dominant role of Islam, the effect of geographical diversity, deeply entrenched social structures, and contemporary societal dynamics collectively shape the multifaceted character of Pakistan. These elements are not only significant in understanding the nation's past but are crucial in determining its future. The richness of Pakistan's cultural heritage, coupled with evolving societal norms, continues to shape its political, economic, and social landscape. The intermingling of tradition and modernity, local and global, individual and community forms a dynamic tapestry, crafting the unique story of Pakistan's evolution and the potential trajectory of its success.

5.2 SOCIOCULTURAL TRIUMPHS: EMBRACING DIVERSITY AND PLURALISM

In a country as ethnically, linguistically, and religiously diverse as Pakistan, embracing diversity is not just a virtue, but an imperative for social harmony and national development. Located at the confluence of South Asia, Central Asia, and the Middle East, Pakistan has inherited an enriching tapestry of cultures, languages, and traditions, making it a veritable mosaic of diversity. From the Pashtuns of Khyber Pakhtunkhwa to the Sindhis of the Indus plains, the diverse ethnic groups contribute to the unique cultural identity of Pakistan. This plurality extends to the religious realm too, where despite the majority being Muslim, it encompasses a variety of sects, alongside minorities such as Christians, Hindus, Sikhs, and others.

Embracing this diversity holds the key to understanding the Pakistani identity, fosters social cohesion, and serves as a bedrock for national progress. By acknowledging and celebrating the various strands of its societal fabric, Pakistan can effectively navigate the complexities of its multicultural landscape. In doing so, it leverages the collective strength of its population towards creating a society where everyone feels included and valued. This chapter delves into the triumphs of Pakistan in embracing its diversity and pluralism, painting a picture of its sociocultural landscape that is as varied as it is vibrant.

Understanding Diversity and Pluralism

Understanding the concepts of diversity and pluralism is fundamental to appreciating the rich sociocultural landscape of Pakistan. Diversity refers to the presence of distinct characteristics within a group, community, or country. It signifies differences in ethnic backgrounds, languages, religious beliefs, and other aspects of human identity. Pluralism, on the other hand, goes a step further. It is the acceptance, recognition, and celebration of these differences. Pluralistic societies are not just diverse, they also foster an environment of respect and tolerance for diversity, allowing various groups to coexist harmoniously.

Pakistan embodies diversity in its truest sense. Ethnically, the country is a tapestry of distinct groups, each with its unique traditions and customs. From the Punjabis, Sindhis, and Balochs to the Pashtuns and Mohajirs, each ethnic group adds to the rich cultural character of Pakistan. This multiplicity of ethnicities gives rise to a stunning array of languages. While Urdu serves as the national language, regional languages such as Punjabi, Sindhi, Pashto, and Balochi, among others, are widely spoken and cherished.

Religion, too, is an integral part of Pakistan's diversity. Predominantly a Muslim country, Pakistan is home to a range of Islamic sects, including Sunni, Shia, and others. This is in addition to the presence of religious minorities, such as Christians, Hindus, Sikhs, and Zoroastrians, who contribute to the pluralistic fabric of Pakistani society.

Embracing this diversity is critical for Pakistan's societal harmony and unity. Acknowledging and cherishing these different identities fosters a sense of belonging and mutual respect among various groups, leading to a more inclusive and cohesive society. However, the road to pluralism is not without its challenges. Balancing the preservation of distinct identities with the promotion of national unity requires constant negotiation and understanding. The following sections will delve deeper into Pakistan's journey towards becoming a truly pluralistic society.

Pakistan's Diverse Cultural Landscape

Pakistan's cultural landscape is a remarkable blend of ethnicities, religions, and traditions, each bringing unique flavours to the country's cultural tapestry.

Ethnic diversity is at the core of the cultural richness in Pakistan. The Punjabis, the largest ethnic group, are known for their vivacious folk dances, such as Bhangra and Luddi, and their hearty cuisine with signature dishes like Nihari and Sarson ka Saag. Sindhis, hailing from the land of the ancient Indus Valley Civilization, are renowned for their embroidered ajrak shawls and Sindhi Biryani. The Pashtuns, rooted in tribal traditions from the rugged mountains of Khyber Pakhtunkhwa and FATA, are famous for their code of Pashtunwali and hospitality, while the distinctive Balochi culture is reflected in their nomadic lifestyle, handicrafts, and Sajji, a popular Balochi dish. The Muhajirs, immigrants from India at the time of partition, have significantly influenced Pakistan's national language, Urdu, contributing to its literature, poetry, and arts.

Language is another aspect of Pakistan's diversity. While Urdu serves as a lingua franca, fostering national unity, over 60 regional languages are spoken across the country. These languages, including Punjabi, Sindhi, Pashto, Balochi, Saraiki, Shina, and Balti, are more than just communication tools. They are cultural carriers, preserving centuries-old traditions, folklore, music, and poetry.

The religious diversity of Pakistan further enriches its cultural tapestry. While a majority of the population practices Islam, the country also provides a home to several minority communities. Christians, Hindus, Sikhs, and Parsis live across the country, each community adding to the cultural diversity with their unique religious practices, festivals, and traditions.

Pakistani culture is also coloured by Sufism, a mystical form of Islam that has flourished in the region for centuries. The shrines of Sufi saints such as Data Ganj Bakhsh in Lahore and Shahbaz Qalandar in Sehwan are significant cultural and religious landmarks, hosting vibrant festivals that draw devotees from various backgrounds.

This rich cultural mosaic has greatly shaped Pakistan's identity, making it a fascinating study of diversity. Each ethnic group, language, and religion is a thread in the vibrant cultural tapestry, their interweaving creating a dynamic, multifaceted society. This diversity is a testament to Pakistan's cultural wealth and resilience, an essential element to understand when exploring the nation's triumphs and trials. As we dive deeper into the implications of this diversity, it becomes clear that the journey towards embracing it is both challenging and rewarding.

Embracing Diversity: Sociocultural Triumphs

The vibrant tapestry of diversity in Pakistan has often been the source of celebration, leading to social triumphs that resonate throughout the nation. This celebration of diversity is not only an acknowledgement of the pluralistic nature of Pakistani society but is also a conscious step towards promoting peace, tolerance, and social harmony.

Multicultural events in Pakistan provide a powerful testament to this spirit of inclusivity. The Lahore Literary Festival, for instance, is a premier cultural event that brings together writers, intellectuals, artists, and enthusiasts from diverse linguistic and ethnic backgrounds. The festival showcases the richness of Pakistan's literary heritage while also exposing attendees to global literary trends. Similarly, the Karachi Biennale, an international contemporary art event, unites artists from across the globe, further fostering an exchange of diverse ideas and cultural practices.

Further evidence of Pakistan's embrace of its diversity is seen in the realm of media and entertainment. Television dramas and films often portray characters from various ethnic and religious communities, highlighting their unique customs and values, while also underscoring shared human experiences. The wildly popular Coke Studio music platform exemplifies this blending of diverse cultural elements, where folk musicians from remote corners of the country share the stage with modern pop artists, creating a unique fusion of traditional and contemporary music.

Interfaith harmony, an essential aspect of societal peace, has been promoted through various initiatives. For instance, the opening of the Kartarpur Corridor, a border corridor between Pakistan and India, has allowed Sikh pilgrims from India to visit one of their holy sites in Pakistan without a visa. This gesture has been lauded internationally for promoting peace and religious tolerance. Similarly, the restoration of Hindu temples and the government's support for the celebration of the Holi and Diwali festivals demonstrate respect for religious diversity.

Policies promoting diversity are also noteworthy. The Pakistani government has made efforts to ensure representation of minority groups in the Parliament and has reserved seats for women to promote gender diversity. Educational policies also encourage the teaching of regional languages and literature, fostering an understanding and appreciation of the country's rich linguistic diversity among young Pakistanis.

Furthermore, various Non-Governmental Organizations (NGOs) have also played a crucial role in promoting diversity. Organizations such as the Citizens Archive of Pakistan work to preserve the diverse cultural heritage of the country, while the Aurat Foundation and Kashf Foundation work towards women's empowerment, striving for a more inclusive society.

Pakistan's journey towards embracing diversity is ongoing and fraught with challenges. However, these instances of triumph, where diversity has been celebrated and has led to positive outcomes, provide a beacon of hope. They underscore the potential that lies in harnessing Pakistan's rich cultural diversity for social progress and national unity. The continued celebration and promotion of this diversity, in all its forms, are indeed key to fostering an environment of tolerance, mutual respect, and peaceful co-existence in Pakistan's pluralistic society.

The Role of Education, Media, and Civil Society

The role of education, media, and civil society is vital in cultivating an environment of diversity and pluralism in any society, and the situation in Pakistan is no different.

The educational sector holds a significant position in fostering a sense of unity in diversity. Schools and universities serve as melting pots where young people from diverse backgrounds interact, learn, and grow together. The incorporation of multicultural education in curriculums, teaching of regional languages, and the inclusion of courses on religious tolerance can contribute greatly to promoting an understanding and appreciation of diversity among the younger generation. Higher education institutions in Pakistan, like the Lahore University of Management Sciences and Quaid-i-Azam University, have increasingly sought to ensure a diverse student body, enriching the learning experience through exposure to varying perspectives and cultural experiences.

The media, with its wide reach and influence, also plays a critical role in shaping public perceptions about diversity. Pakistan's media landscape, which includes television, radio, print, and digital media, has been instrumental in highlighting the country's rich cultural heritage. Television dramas often depict the lives of different ethnic and religious communities, fostering empathy and understanding among viewers. Music platforms like Coke Studio have done commendable work in bridging cultural divides, blending folk traditions from different regions with contemporary music styles, thereby presenting a harmonious image of Pakistan's cultural diversity.

Civil society organizations, too, have a significant role in championing diversity and pluralism. Non-Governmental Organizations (NGOs), like the Citizens Archive of Pakistan, work tirelessly to preserve the cultural and historical diversity of Pakistan. Similarly, organizations like the Human Rights Commission of Pakistan and the Aurat Foundation play an important role in advocating for the rights of minority groups and women, striving for a more inclusive society.

Efforts to promote interfaith harmony, such as those by the Interfaith Harmony Council, which organizes interfaith dialogues and conferences, play an essential part in fostering a climate of religious tolerance. Similarly, initiatives such as the Pakistan-India People's Forum for Peace and Democracy work at the grassroots level to promote peace and understanding between the two countries, underscoring the value of dialogue and human connection over divisive politics.

In conclusion, the sectors of education, media, and civil society are instrumental in promoting diversity and pluralism within Pakistan. By shaping perceptions, fostering understanding, and advocating for inclusivity, they contribute significantly to the country's sociocultural triumphs. The collective efforts of these sectors will continue to be crucial in navigating the path towards a more inclusive and harmonious future for Pakistan.

Conclusion

In conclusion, the multitude of cultures, languages, and traditions that reside within Pakistan's borders enrich the country's societal fabric. This chapter underscored the abundant cultural and societal diversity of Pakistan, highlighted instances where the embrace of this diversity has resulted in positive outcomes, and outlined the crucial role of education, media, and civil society in promoting pluralism.

However, the celebration of diversity should not merely be an exception, but rather a norm. Recognizing the sociocultural triumphs is only the starting point. For Pakistan to continue its progress on the path to inclusivity and harmony, embracing diversity and pluralism should be integral to its national ethos. It necessitates concerted efforts from all stakeholders, from the government implementing inclusive policies, to educational institutions promoting multicultural understanding, to media houses responsibly representing all ethnicities and sects.

Initiatives like diversity training programs, awareness campaigns, and interfaith dialogues can significantly contribute to fostering a culture of acceptance and respect. Furthermore, including diverse voices in decision-making processes at all levels can help ensure a more inclusive society.

By harnessing its diversity, Pakistan can build a more cohesive, inclusive, and resilient society. The country's success hinges on its ability to not just accept, but celebrate its multifaceted diversity, turning pluralism from a challenge into an opportunity. The future of Pakistan as a prosperous and unified nation rests on its commitment to uphold and cherish this diverse heritage, which is truly its strength.

5.3 SOCIOCULTURAL CHALLENGES AND THEIR IMPLICATIONS FOR PROGRESS

The exploration of sociocultural challenges in Pakistan is essential for gaining a comprehensive understanding of the country's path towards development and progress. This chapter aims to delve into the intricate tapestry of Pakistani society and culture, unearthing the myriad challenges that emerge from the societal norms, practices, and structures inherent to the nation. These sociocultural challenges, although seemingly embedded in the fabric of everyday life, hold profound implications for the country's trajectory, shaping the contours of social, economic, and political landscapes.

From entrenched social inequality to rising religious intolerance, from glaring gender disparities to simmering ethnic tensions, Pakistan navigates through a complex sociocultural labyrinth. This maze, often, hampers the realization of the country's full potential, stifling the aspirations of its populace and restraining the pace of national advancement. Consequently, the necessity to understand, address, and surmount these challenges is not merely an intellectual exercise but a crucial prerequisite for fostering an inclusive, prosperous, and harmonious Pakistan.

Through the lens of this chapter, we aim to elucidate these multifaceted challenges, unravel their implications for Pakistan's progress, and contribute to the discourse on potential pathways towards their resolution. This exercise is not just about diagnosing societal predicaments but also about envisioning a future that leverages the strength of diversity and the spirit of pluralism for a resilient Pakistan.

Understanding Sociocultural Challenges

Sociocultural challenges, as the term implies, refer to the social and cultural obstacles that societies face in their pursuit of progress and development. These challenges are deeply rooted in societal norms, practices, and structures that shape individual and collective behaviours, decision-making processes, and societal relations. Often, these sociocultural issues are so embedded in society that they become part of the everyday experiences of individuals, impacting their opportunities, rights, and social interactions.

For Pakistan, a country characterized by its cultural richness and social diversity, sociocultural challenges pose significant hurdles. From social inequalities rooted in class, caste, gender, and ethnic lines, to cultural practices that perpetuate discrimination and violence, these issues permeate various spheres of Pakistani society. A few key sociocultural challenges in Pakistan encompass rigid social hierarchies, gender-based discrimination, religious intolerance, and regional disparities.

Social hierarchies in Pakistan, often reinforced by feudalistic land relations and tribal affiliations, perpetuate disparities in wealth and power distribution. Gender-based discrimination, manifested through patriarchal norms, societal attitudes, and even legislation, impedes women's empowerment, limiting their access to education, healthcare, and economic opportunities.

Religious intolerance, a rising concern in Pakistan, manifests through discrimination against religious minorities, sectarian violence, and misuse of blasphemy laws. This intolerance often leads to social unrest, infringements on minority rights, and impediments to social cohesion.

Finally, regional disparities, often along ethnic lines, result in uneven development and access to resources across the country. These disparities fuel ethnic tensions and separatist movements, undermining national unity and social stability.

Each of these sociocultural challenges, while distinct in nature, is intertwined, amplifying each other's impacts. They serve as roadblocks to Pakistan's development, impinging upon social justice, economic growth, and political stability. Thus, understanding these challenges is crucial to devising strategies for Pakistan's progress, a journey that requires transforming societal structures and norms towards more inclusive and equitable paradigms.

In-Depth Examination of Key Challenges

Social Inequality

Social inequality in Pakistan is a deeply ingrained challenge rooted in class, caste, and feudal structures. The Gini coefficient, a measure of income inequality, stands significantly high, indicating a wide chasm between the rich and poor. The feudalistic land ownership structure and the caste system further compound the issue, concentrating wealth and power in the hands of a small elite and perpetuating cycles of poverty and disenfranchisement among the lower classes. This economic inequality restricts access to resources, opportunities, and social mobility for a large segment of the population. It also exacerbates other social problems, such as crime, health disparities, and educational inequality. On a macro level, persistent social inequality poses serious threats to social cohesion and economic development, leading to social unrest and a stagnant human development index.

Gender Disparities

Despite constitutional guarantees of gender equality, Pakistan grapples with substantial gender disparities. Discriminatory societal attitudes, patriarchal norms, and restrictive cultural practices limit women's access to education, employment, and health services. Additionally, issues such as gender-based violence, child marriage, and honour crimes remain prevalent. Women's labour force participation rate is significantly lower than men's, and the female literacy rate lags behind. Such gender disparities not only violate women's rights but also impede economic development by underutilizing half of the country's potential human capital. Furthermore, the unequal power dynamics perpetuated by gender disparities lead to societal imbalances that can breed violence and instability.

Religious Intolerance

Religious intolerance, manifested in sectarian violence, discrimination against religious minorities, and misuse of blasphemy laws, is a growing concern in Pakistan. While Islam is the state religion, Pakistan is home to diverse religious communities, including Christians, Hindus, Sikhs, and several Muslim sects. Increasingly, religious minorities face discrimination, violence, and legal disadvantages, undermining social harmony and human rights. Sectarian violence, primarily between Sunni and Shia communities, further compounds religious intolerance. This growing religious intolerance threatens social cohesion, fuels violence, and hampers attempts at political stabilization.

Ethnic Tensions

Pakistan is a multi-ethnic state, comprising several ethnic groups, including Punjabis, Sindhis, Pashtuns, Baloch, Muhajirs, and many more. However, ethnic tensions, often tied to regional disparities in development and resource allocation, have posed significant challenges to national unity. Tensions have historically been particularly high in Balochistan and Sindh provinces, with occasional outbreaks of violence and separatist movements. These tensions reflect the struggle for power and resources, linguistic and cultural differences, and feelings of marginalization among ethnic minorities. The resulting discord hampers social integration, destabilizes political structures, and impairs economic growth by fuelling conflict and instability. Thus, resolving ethnic tensions is critical for achieving peaceful progress in Pakistan.

Implications for Progress

These sociocultural challenges collectively pose severe obstacles to Pakistan's progress, reaching far beyond their immediate social impacts to deeply affect the country's economic growth, political stability, and international standing.

Social inequality, with its roots entrenched in centuries-old feudalistic and caste structures, perpetuates a cycle of poverty that is tough to break. This entrenched inequality hampers economic development by creating an enormous wealth gap and limiting opportunities for the lower classes. It reduces social mobility and creates barriers to quality education and healthcare, keeping a significant portion of the population in poverty. The World Bank indicates that economic inequality can slow down poverty reduction and economic growth. In the case of Pakistan, it exacerbates social tensions and creates a volatile environment that can deter foreign investment.

Gender disparities in Pakistan result in an underutilization of human capital, which is a critical setback for a developing economy. Women represent nearly half of Pakistan's population, yet their potential remains largely untapped due to cultural norms, discrimination, and limited access to resources. The World Economic Forum's Global Gender Gap Report ranks Pakistan near the bottom, signifying a vast gender disparity in economic participation and opportunity. Closing this gender gap could yield enormous dividends, including increased economic productivity, a diversified workforce, improved family health, and more inclusive growth.

Religious intolerance and ethnic tensions undermine social cohesion, leading to violence, instability, and a lack of trust among different communities. They also negatively affect Pakistan's political landscape, where sectarian or ethnic identities often become the basis for political mobilization. Prolonged periods of violence and unrest can deter investment, disrupt economic activities, and drain public resources. According to a study by the Institute for Economics and Peace, religious and ethnic conflicts can reduce GDP growth rate by hampering economic activities, diverting public resources, and causing physical destruction.

Moreover, these sociocultural challenges can impact Pakistan's international reputation, affecting diplomatic relations and potential partnerships. They also exacerbate Pakistan's human rights record, impacting its international standing and potentially influencing decisions of foreign investors and international funding agencies.

In essence, the sociocultural challenges facing Pakistan not only affect the immediate well-being and rights of its citizens but also have profound implications for the nation's long-term stability and prosperity. Overcoming these challenges will require concerted efforts at all societal levels, backed by progressive policy measures and inclusive governance.

Policy Measures and Potential Solutions

Addressing the deeply rooted sociocultural challenges Pakistan faces requires a comprehensive, multi-pronged approach that involves the government, civil society, and ordinary citizens alike.

Policies that promote equal opportunities and address systemic injustices can go a long way in alleviating social inequality. These can include land reform, progressive taxation, and investment in public services such as education and healthcare, particularly in underserved areas. To ensure the effectiveness of these measures, transparent implementation and stringent anti-corruption practices are key.

Combatting gender disparities requires not only protective legislation but also societal change. Enhancing female participation in education, particularly in STEM fields, and promoting women's entry into the workforce are important steps. Simultaneously, social awareness campaigns can help challenge deep-seated patriarchal norms and attitudes.

Addressing religious intolerance and ethnic tensions necessitates an inclusive national narrative that celebrates diversity and promotes pluralism. This can be achieved through reforms in educational curricula, fostering interfaith and interethnic dialogue, and implementing stringent laws against hate speech and violence.

Crucially, these efforts need to be underpinned by a strong political will and an active civil society advocating for change. Pakistan's progress towards overcoming its sociocultural challenges hinges on collective responsibility and action.

Conclusion

In conclusion, Pakistan's sociocultural landscape, though rich and diverse, is riddled with significant challenges including social inequality, gender disparities, religious intolerance, and ethnic tensions. These hurdles not only impact the daily lives of the citizenry but also impede the nation's progress across economic, political, and social dimensions. Addressing these issues requires transformative policies, societal shifts, and concerted efforts from all sectors of society. As the nation moves forward, it is crucial to recognize and tackle these challenges, laying the groundwork for an inclusive, equitable, and progressive Pakistan.

6. EDUCATION AND LITERACY

6.1 EDUCATION IN PAKISTAN: A HISTORICAL OVERVIEW

Education is a fundamental pillar of societal growth, economic development, and nation-building. It is a powerful tool for reducing poverty, fostering social equality, and promoting peaceful coexistence. In the context of Pakistan, a country with a burgeoning youth population and immense potential, the role of education becomes even more critical. This chapter seeks to explore the historical evolution of education in Pakistan, tracing its journey from pre-independence times to the present day.

The development of Pakistan's educational landscape has been influenced by a myriad of socio-political factors. Understanding these historic trajectories is crucial to grasping the successes and challenges of the present system. This exploration will provide a comprehensive understanding of how historical circumstances, political decisions, cultural elements, and economic factors have collectively shaped the education sector in Pakistan. Thus, this chapter aims to paint a detailed picture of the educational tapestry of Pakistan, setting the stage for a thoughtful discussion on the way forward.

Pre-Independence Era

Prior to the establishment of Pakistan, the region was under British colonial rule, which significantly shaped the contours of its educational landscape. The British colonial administration introduced a formal education system in the subcontinent that was geared primarily towards producing an English-speaking bureaucratic class to assist in the administration of the colony.

The education system under the British Raj was characterized by a sharp dichotomy. On one hand, there was the traditional education prevalent among the Muslim populace, which was primarily religious, delivered in Madrassas and centered around Islamic teachings. On the other hand, the British introduced Western-style education, taught in English, and focused heavily on the humanities and sciences. This system, though accessible to a limited population, was instrumental in creating a new class of English-educated elites.

However, the majority of the population had limited access to this Western education, leading to a significant disparity in the educational attainment of different segments of society. The divide also had a strong communal dimension, with Muslim communities particularly underrepresented in the new education system. This was due to a variety of factors, including socio-economic constraints, geographical barriers, and apprehensions about the secular orientation of the British education system.

This state of affairs had significant repercussions on the development of education post-independence. The new country inherited an educational system that was skewed towards urban areas, featured a strong emphasis on rote learning, and had a significant English-medium bias. These characteristics have continued to influence the shape and direction of Pakistan's education system in the years that followed independence.

Post-Independence Era

The dawn of independence in 1947 brought with it an urgent need for Pakistan to develop its own education system that would cater to the needs of the nascent state. The initial years were marked by numerous challenges such as scarcity of resources, shortage of trained teachers, and the need to accommodate refugees who migrated during partition.

The first decade of independence witnessed a focus on

expanding educational opportunities for the Pakistani populace. However, there was a major challenge - the inherited system was English-medium, thus catering to a small, urban, elite section of society. This led to the adoption of the policy of Urdu as the national language in 1954 and its subsequent implementation as a medium of instruction in schools. This move, intended to democratize education, faced hurdles due to the multilingual nature of Pakistani society and the lack of resources for the translation of educational material.

The 1959 report of the Commission on National Education, also known as the Sharif Commission, was a major milestone in the history of education in Pakistan. The Commission recommended free and compulsory education, a uniform education system, and increased emphasis on technical and vocational training. However, the implementation of these recommendations was lacklustre due to resource constraints and political instability.

The period also saw the establishment of key educational institutions, such as the University of Karachi in 1951 and the University of Peshawar in 1950. These universities served as crucial educational hubs, catering to the higher education needs of the population.

In summary, the post-independence era was marked by both challenges and opportunities. Although the Pakistani government took steps to create an inclusive education system, constraints of resources and political instability hampered the process. Nevertheless, this period laid the foundation of the education system in Pakistan, with efforts to extend education to every citizen and attempts to localize and nationalize the system inherited from the British Raj.

Education in the Bhutto and Zia Era (1971-1988)

The Bhutto and Zia eras (1971-1988) brought significant

changes to the education system in Pakistan, primarily through Bhutto's nationalization policies and Zia's Islamization drive. These policies left a lasting imprint on Pakistan's educational landscape.

When Zulfikar Ali Bhutto assumed power in 1971, he embarked on an ambitious plan to restructure Pakistan's education system. In 1972, Bhutto launched a major educational reform with the nationalization of private schools and colleges. The rationale behind this move was to create a more egalitarian and uniform education system, bridging the gap between rich and poor. Nationalization aimed at breaking the monopoly of private schools, which were often accused of catering only to the elites. It was expected that bringing schools under state control would make education accessible and affordable for all.

However, the policy did not yield the desired results. With state takeover, the quality of education declined due to bureaucratic inefficiencies and lack of resources. The nationalized schools and colleges suffered from inadequate funding, outdated curricula, and a shortage of qualified teachers. The policy received widespread criticism, leading to a gradual de-nationalization process in the following decades.

General Zia-ul-Haq's era ushered in a different kind of educational reform, the Islamization of education. Following the 1979 Islamic Revolution in Iran and in an attempt to legitimize his military rule, Zia initiated a policy of Islamization across all sectors of society, including education. School curricula were revised to include more Islamic studies, and 'Islamic Ideology' was made a compulsory subject. Madrassahs (religious schools) received state patronage during this period. However, critics argue that the heavy emphasis on religious education led to a neglect of subjects like science and mathematics, adversely affecting the quality and breadth of education.

Overall, the Bhutto and Zia eras marked significant shifts in

Pakistan's education policy. While both leaders aimed to restructure the education system in line with their political ideologies, the policies implemented during their tenure had mixed outcomes and continue to shape the educational landscape of Pakistan today.

Post-Zia Era (1988-Present)

The period following General Zia-ul-Haq's rule has been marked by an increased recognition of the importance of education for national development and efforts to reform the education system. Since 1988, various governments have attempted to address the gaps in education, and while challenges persist, there have been notable improvements.

Under Benazir Bhutto's two non-consecutive tenures as Prime Minister (1988-1990 and 1993-1996), the government introduced significant reforms aimed at modernizing the education system. These included updating the national curriculum, expanding female education, and implementing teacher training programs. However, these efforts were hampered by political instability and economic difficulties.

The era of General Pervez Musharraf (1999-2008), who seized power in a military coup, saw increased focus on education. His government significantly increased the budgetary allocation for education. In 2001, the government unveiled a comprehensive National Education Policy, aiming to improve literacy rates, enhance the quality of education, and promote gender parity. Furthermore, technical, and vocational training programs were strengthened to boost employment opportunities for young people.

The post-Musharraf period has seen a shift towards decentralization in the education sector following the 18th Constitutional Amendment in 2010, which devolved education to the provinces. This has led to increased diversity in education policies across different provinces, each trying to cater to their unique needs.

Moreover, this period has seen an increased role of international donors and non-governmental organizations (NGOs) in the education sector. Bodies like USAID, the World Bank, and the UK's Department for International Development (DFID) have provided significant financial and technical support to Pakistan's education sector. Their initiatives have covered a wide array of areas, from infrastructure development and teacher training to curriculum reform and school management.

Similarly, numerous local and international NGOs have played an active role in supplementing government efforts to improve education. They have filled critical gaps, such as setting up schools in remote areas, providing free or subsidized education, and implementing innovative teaching methods.

Imran Khan & Education

Imran Khan, the former Prime Minister of Pakistan, identified education reform as a central theme of his government. His initial 100-day agenda sought to "revolutionise social services", including transforming health and education.

One of Khan's key education reforms was the introduction of a Single National Curriculum (SNC). The SNC was a unified curriculum for all schools in Pakistan, regardless of their public or private status. It was designed to promote national unity and cohesion, as well as to improve the quality of education across the country.

In addition to the SNC, Khan's government also launched a number of other education initiatives, including increasing the education budget, providing free textbooks and uniforms to students, expanding access to technical and vocational education, and most importantly, reforming the madrassa education system. Khan's government also made significant progress in increasing enrolment rates and reducing gender disparities in education.

Despite these efforts, Pakistan's education system still faces major challenges, including low enrolment rates, high dropout rates, gender disparity, poor quality of education, and inadequate infrastructure. Addressing these issues is crucial to harness the full potential of Pakistan's large youth population, and thus, remains an important task for policymakers.

Current State of Education

As of now, Pakistan's education system presents a mixed picture of progress and challenges. The country has made significant strides in expanding access to education, with a noticeable increase in enrolment rates, particularly for girls, and literacy rates have also improved. There have been advancements in the higher education sector with the establishment of world-class universities and research institutions. However, the system is still grappling with issues like high dropout rates, disparities in access to quality education between urban and rural areas and across different income levels, outdated curricula, and inadequately trained teachers, which need urgent attention for holistic improvement.

Conclusion

The historical journey of Pakistan's education system has been complex and multifaceted, deeply intertwined with the political, social, and cultural realities of each era. From the initial struggles in the post-independence era to the nationalization policies of Bhutto and the Islamization drive under Zia, each phase has left an indelible imprint on the country's educational infrastructure and philosophy. In recent years, we have seen commendable efforts to enhance accessibility, particularly for marginalized communities, and to uplift the standard of higher education. However, persistent issues related to quality, equity, and systemic inefficiencies continue to pose significant challenges. Understanding this historical trajectory is not just an academic exercise but a critical prerequisite for devising effective future strategies. It offers invaluable lessons for policymakers, allowing them to replicate successes, avoid past mistakes, and ensure that education in Pakistan evolves to meet the changing needs of its people and contributes robustly towards national development.

6.2 CURRENT CHALLENGES IN PAKISTAN'S EDUCATION SYSTEM

Education forms the backbone of any nation, shaping its human capital, driving economic growth, and fostering social progress. In the case of Pakistan, a country with a burgeoning youth population, a well-functioning education system is not just a desirable aim; it is a critical necessity. Over the years, the country has striven to uplift its education sector, undertaking various reforms and initiatives to expand access, improve quality, and promote equity. These efforts have yielded certain progress, as seen in increased enrolment rates, improved gender parity, and the expansion of higher education.

Yet, the Pakistani education system continues to grapple with a multitude of complex and multifaceted challenges. These issues span the spectrum from infrastructural deficits and quality concerns to deep-seated social disparities and policy lacunas. The resolution of these challenges is a daunting task but one that is indispensable for Pakistan's future. This chapter delves into an exploration of these pressing educational issues, underscoring the imperative of concerted action and sustainable solutions.

Overview of the Education System

Pakistan's education system is divided into five main levels: Pre-primary, Primary, Middle, High, and Higher Secondary/Intermediate. After these five levels, tertiary education at universities or colleges is offered.

Pre-primary education serves as the foundation of the learning process and includes children from ages 3 to 5. Primary education comprises grades one through five, serving students aged 5-9. Middle school is for students aged 10-12 and encompasses grades six through eight. High school education, for students aged 13-14, includes ninth and tenth grades. The higher secondary or intermediate level covers eleventh and twelfth grades, catering to students aged 15-16.

Tertiary education, comprising bachelor's, master's, and doctoral degrees, is provided by universities and degree colleges. There are also technical and vocational education institutions offering skill-based training.

The education system is primarily bifurcated into public (government-run) and private sectors. The public sector, while reaching a larger population, often suffers from issues of quality, infrastructure, and resource allocation. On the other hand, private education in Pakistan, known for its relatively higher quality, is usually costly, making it inaccessible to a large portion of the population.

Statistically, Pakistan has made some strides in education over the years, yet it lags in many areas. The net enrolment rate for primary education is around 57%, but it declines significantly for secondary and tertiary levels. Furthermore, the dropout rate is a serious issue, with nearly 22.8 million children out of school, representing the world's second-highest number of out-of-school children.

Gender parity is another significant concern, with girls having lower access to education, especially in rural areas. The literacy rate for females is considerably lower than for males, underscoring the gender divide in education. Despite an official policy to maintain a student-teacher ratio of 40:1, many public schools, particularly in rural areas, far exceed this ratio, which negatively impacts the quality of education.

In sum, while the structure of Pakistan's education system is comparable to global standards, its performance is marred by various challenges that hamper the achievement of educational goals.

Detailed Analysis of Key Challenges

Access to Education

Access to education remains a pressing issue in Pakistan. Approximately 22.8 million children are not in school, constituting the world's second-highest number of out-of-school children. The lack of access is particularly prominent in rural areas due to factors like a shortage of schools, long distances to schools, and safety concerns, especially for girls. Besides, the cost of education, including indirect costs like uniforms and transportation, poses a significant barrier for many families. Government efforts such as the introduction of a nationwide school enrolment drive have sought to address these challenges. However, consistent efforts are required to overcome the infrastructural deficiencies, societal norms, and financial constraints that obstruct educational access.

Quality of Education

Even when children can access schooling, the quality of education often remains inadequate. Overcrowded classrooms, insufficient learning materials, and poorly trained or absent teachers characterize many schools, especially in the public sector. This issue is reflected in the learning outcomes; a large number of students lack proficiency in foundational skills like reading and mathematics. For instance, according to the Annual Status of Education Report (ASER), nearly half of grade 5 students cannot read a grade 2-level story in local languages. Improving quality, therefore, necessitates investment in teacher training, infrastructural development, and accountability mechanisms.

Inequality in Education

Education in Pakistan also exhibits stark disparities based on location (rural vs. urban), gender, and socioeconomic status. Rural areas, in particular, are disadvantaged due to inadequate school facilities, a shortage of teachers, and high dropout rates. Gender disparities exist in terms of enrolment and literacy rates, with societal norms and security issues limiting girls' education, especially in conservative and conflict-affected regions. The children of poorer families, likewise, have lower educational participation due to financial constraints and the opportunity cost of schooling. Thus, targeted interventions are needed to overcome these entrenched inequalities and ensure education for all.

Insufficient Funding

Pakistan spends only about 2.3% of its GDP on education, significantly lower than the recommended UNESCO benchmark of 4-6%. This underfunding leads to infrastructural deficits, a shortage of teaching resources, and low teacher salaries, impacting both access and quality. Despite a commitment to enhance education funding, progress has been slow and inconsistent, owing to competing fiscal demands and implementation challenges at the provincial level.

Outdated Curriculum

The curriculum in many Pakistani schools is often outdated, lacking in practical skills, and biased towards rote learning. This restricts the development of critical thinking, creativity, and problem-solving abilities among students. Furthermore, the curriculum's content has been criticized for promoting intolerance and not adequately addressing the country's diverse history and culture. Various curriculum reforms have been initiated, but their effective implementation remains a challenge due to a lack of resources, teacher training, and resistance from certain quarters. Therefore, a comprehensive and inclusive curriculum reform, coupled with a shift towards student-centered pedagogy, is critical for preparing Pakistani students for the demands of the 21st century.

Implications of these Challenges

The current challenges in Pakistan's education system carry significant implications for the country's social and economic development. Human capital development, a critical driver of economic growth, is undermined by the combination of low school enrolment, high dropout rates, and poor education quality. With an undereducated population, Pakistan struggles to increase productivity, innovation, and competitiveness in a global economy that increasingly values knowledge and skills.

The challenges in education also exacerbate social inequality. Disparities in educational access and attainment based on location, gender, and socioeconomic status reproduce and reinforce existing patterns of social and economic inequality. Those without access to quality education are more likely to remain trapped in a cycle of poverty, with limited opportunities for upward social mobility.

Further, these educational challenges threaten social cohesion and stability. The absence of inclusive and quality education can contribute to social resentment, facilitate the spread of extremist ideologies, and discourage civic participation. A poor education system also undermines the nation's ability to cultivate informed and engaged citizens capable of contributing to democratic governance and social progress.

Overall, these challenges present a formidable obstacle to Pakistan's pursuit of sustainable development, underscoring the urgent need for comprehensive education reform.

Conclusion

In conclusion, the education system in Pakistan faces a plethora of challenges, including lack of access, poor quality of education, educational inequality, insufficient funding, and an outdated curriculum. These issues hold profound implications for the country's social and economic development, as they impede human capital formation, perpetuate social inequality, and compromise social cohesion. Addressing these challenges is of paramount importance for Pakistan to ensure its future progress and prosperity. Through proactive policymaking and implementation, it is crucial to transform these challenges into opportunities for a brighter, more inclusive future for the country's youth and, consequently, for the nation as a whole.

6.3 THE POWER OF EDUCATION: SHAPING THE FUTURE

Education stands as a transformative force capable of redefining the trajectory of a nation. In the context of Pakistan, a country brimming with potential and teeming with a youthful population, education plays a particularly pivotal role in shaping the nation's destiny. This chapter delves into the power of education, examining how it underpins economic prosperity, instigates social change, consolidates political stability, and paves the way for a sustainable future. It provides a cogent argument for investing in education, not just as a fundamental right of every individual, but also as a catalyst for holistic and inclusive development in Pakistan.

The Potential of Education: Economic, Social, and Political Impacts

Education is the bedrock of societal transformation and progress. Its potential transcends the confines of traditional classroom learning, extending into the realms of economic development, social change, and political stability, forming the foundation of a prosperous nation.

From an economic standpoint, education fuels growth by

honing the most crucial asset for a nation's development: its human capital. It equips individuals with the skills and knowledge needed to participate in the economy effectively and adapt to the fast-paced, evolving world of work. For instance, a well-educated workforce fosters innovation, boosts productivity, and promotes entrepreneurship, collectively driving economic advancement. Additionally, education opens the doors to better job opportunities, contributing to individual economic prosperity and reducing poverty levels. In Pakistan, a country aiming to uplift its economic profile, fostering a robust education system is the key to unlocking its untapped economic potential.

Socially, education acts as a catalyst for change, shaping societal norms and values. It encourages critical thinking, promotes social awareness, and instils a sense of civic responsibility. It enlightens individuals about their rights and responsibilities, fostering a society based on equality and mutual respect. For example, education plays a significant role in promoting gender equality by empowering women, fostering their independence, and challenging patriarchal norms. Furthermore, education raises awareness about pressing global issues such as climate change, reinforcing the importance of sustainable practices. In the context of Pakistan, with its diverse and complex societal fabric, education can bridge cultural and ethnic divides, fostering a more inclusive and tolerant society.

Politically, education underpins stable governance and democracy. An educated populace is more likely to participate in political processes, voice their opinions, and hold leaders accountable, thereby fostering democratic values. It encourages transparent governance by curbing corruption, as a well-informed public is less likely to fall prey to corrupt practices. Moreover, education promotes peace and stability by reducing social tensions and conflicts. For Pakistan, grappling with political instability and governance challenges, education offers a path towards consolidating democracy and fostering a politically stable environment.

In essence, the power of education is transformative, with far-reaching implications for the economic, social, and political landscape of a country. It is, therefore, an investment in the future, capable of catalysing progress and prosperity for Pakistan.

Education for a Sustainable Future

Education is an indispensable tool for fostering sustainable development. It is intrinsically linked to addressing global challenges such as climate change, social inequality, and global health threats, offering solutions that can sustainably transform societies.

Sustainable Development Goals and Education

Education forms an integral part of the United Nations' Sustainable Development Goals (SDGs), reflected in Goal 4: Quality Education. It underscores the importance of inclusive and equitable quality education for all, recognizing it as a fundamental right and a significant contributor to achieving other SDGs. Education equips individuals with the knowledge and skills necessary to promote sustainable development. For instance, it can help alleviate poverty (Goal 1) by boosting employment opportunities, promote gender equality (Goal 5) by empowering women, and nurture innovation (Goal 9) by fostering critical thinking skills. In the context of Pakistan, leveraging education to achieve SDGs could serve as a roadmap to inclusive and sustainable progress.

Education for Environmental Sustainability

Education plays a crucial role in environmental sustainability by raising awareness about the impacts of human actions on the environment and promoting sustainable practices. It teaches individuals to appreciate the value of natural resources, understand the importance of biodiversity, and recognize the urgency of climate action. Environmental education encourages sustainable behaviours such as recycling, energy conservation, and responsible consumption, essential for mitigating environmental degradation and promoting a sustainable future. Moreover, it fosters critical thinking about complex environmental issues, inspiring innovative solutions to combat climate change. For Pakistan, a country increasingly bearing the brunt of climate change impacts, integrating environmental sustainability in education can be a powerful tool to address these challenges and build a greener future.

Conclusion

In conclusion, the power of education extends beyond individual development, playing a pivotal role in shaping the trajectory of nations. In the context of Pakistan, education stands as a cornerstone for economic growth, social transformation, and political stability. By enhancing human capital, it can fuel economic development, promote social equity, and cultivate a well-informed citizenry that can contribute positively to the democratic process.

Moreover, education is key to achieving sustainable development and addressing global challenges such as climate change, social inequality, and health crises. It serves as a conduit for achieving the Sustainable Development Goals and promoting environmental sustainability. Through quality education, individuals can acquire the necessary knowledge, skills, and attitudes to devise sustainable solutions for a rapidly changing world.

Harnessing the power of education is, therefore, an imperative for Pakistan's future progress. The investment in education will pay dividends not only in terms of individual advancement but also in the holistic and sustainable development of the country. Overcoming the challenges in the education sector and capitalizing on its potential should be a top priority for all stakeholders, as Pakistan navigates its path towards a prosperous and sustainable future.

7. HEALTHCARE AND WELLBEING

7.1 HEALTHCARE IN PAKISTAN: THE CURRENT STATE

The healthcare system is a fundamental pillar of any society, playing a crucial role in ensuring the well-being of the population, and thereby directly influencing a nation's productivity and overall development. When examining the context of Pakistan, a developing country with a diverse population of over 220 million, healthcare is not just a matter of individual wellness, but also a significant determinant of the nation's progress. This chapter aims to delve into the intricacies of the Pakistani healthcare system, presenting an overview of its structure, resources, and outcomes. We will further explore the primary health indicators, providing a data-driven snapshot of the nation's health status. The discussion will also highlight the inherent challenges faced by Pakistan's healthcare system, offering a comprehensive understanding of its current state. By laying out this foundation, we set the stage for subsequent discussions on potential improvement strategies and the roadmap to healthcare reforms in Pakistan.

Overview of the Healthcare System

Pakistan's healthcare system is a complex and multifaceted entity, encompassing both public and private sectors. Each sector carries its distinct characteristics and plays a critical role in the overall health service delivery.

The public healthcare system is primarily funded by the government and is structured in a hierarchical manner. It spans from basic health units at the grassroots level, rural health centers and Tehsil headquarter hospitals at the sub-district level, district headquarter hospitals at the district level, to tertiary care hospitals at the provincial level. This tiered structure is designed to cater to the healthcare needs of Pakistan's vast and diverse population, though disparities in access and quality persist across regions.

In contrast, the private healthcare sector is primarily fee-for-service, offering services ranging from small clinics to large, specialized hospitals. The sector's growth has been phenomenal over the years, partly due to perceived gaps in public healthcare, such as long wait times, staff shortages, and lack of advanced equipment.

In addition to modern medicine, traditional and complementary medicine, such as Unani and homeopathic practices, also have a considerable presence in Pakistan. Despite regulatory challenges, they remain popular, particularly in rural areas, due to cultural beliefs and lack of accessibility to allopathic medicine.

Concerning human resources, the healthcare workforce in Pakistan includes doctors, nurses, midwives, pharmacists, paramedics, and community health workers, among others. However, Pakistan faces a significant shortfall in its health workforce. According to the World Health Organization, the doctor-patient ratio is lower than the recommended standards, and the nurse-doctor ratio is heavily skewed in favour of doctors, suggesting a severe shortage of nursing staff. The distribution of healthcare workers is also uneven, with urban areas attracting more professionals than rural areas due to better facilities and opportunities. This imbalance further complicates the healthcare delivery in rural areas, where the majority of Pakistan's population resides.

Healthcare Infrastructure and Resources

The healthcare infrastructure in Pakistan consists of an array of physical assets, including hospitals, clinics, laboratories, pharmacies, and medical equipment. As of the latest data available, Pakistan has a mix of public and private hospitals, including general hospitals, specialized hospitals, rural health centers, basic health units, and dispensaries.

Despite these facilities, the country struggles with a severe shortage and uneven distribution of healthcare resources. The majority of healthcare facilities, especially tertiary care hospitals, are concentrated in urban areas, leaving rural populations underserved. Even within cities, the distribution is uneven with upscale neighbourhoods having more facilities compared to poorer districts.

Moreover, there are stark differences in the quality of healthcare infrastructure across regions. In urban areas, some private hospitals are well-equipped with the latest medical technology, while public hospitals and rural healthcare centers often lack essential medical equipment and infrastructure.

Rural areas rely heavily on basic health units and rural health centers. However, these facilities often suffer from a lack of resources, including medical supplies, electricity, clean water, and well-functioning buildings. As a result, access to quality healthcare services is a significant challenge for people residing in these areas. Additionally, the lack of road infrastructure and transportation in some regions can further hinder access to healthcare facilities.

Another critical aspect of healthcare resources is the availability of essential drugs and medicines. While private pharmacies and hospitals usually have a steady supply of medicines, public healthcare centers often face stockouts, impacting the treatment of patients.

Moreover, in the realm of diagnostic and treatment equipment, there is a scarcity of high-tech devices, especially in the public sector. Advanced equipment like MRI machines, CT scanners, and even basic life-support systems are often concentrated in larger urban hospitals.

The shortage and misallocation of healthcare resources in Pakistan have severe implications for the equitable delivery of healthcare services. Bridging these gaps should be a priority to ensure universal access to quality healthcare.

Health Indicators and Outcomes

Health indicators are statistical measures that provide insights into the health status of a population and the effectiveness of a healthcare system. When we look at the health indicators for Pakistan, they shed light on the considerable health challenges the country is currently facing.

One of the most common health indicators is life expectancy, a measure that estimates the average number of years a person can expect to live. As of the most recent data available, the average life expectancy in Pakistan is lower than the global average, indicating ongoing health issues and shortcomings in healthcare provision.

Infant and maternal mortality rates are other significant indicators that directly reflect the quality of prenatal and postnatal healthcare services. Despite gradual improvements, Pakistan's infant and maternal mortality rates remain high, underscoring challenges in prenatal care, birthing conditions, and neonatal care.

Disease prevalence is also a crucial health indicator. Non-communicable diseases, such as heart disease, cancer, diabetes, and respiratory diseases, account for a substantial proportion of deaths in Pakistan. On the other hand, communicable diseases like tuberculosis, dengue fever, hepatitis, and diarrhoea continue to persist, particularly due to inadequate sanitation and limited access to clean water.

Moreover, Pakistan still battles high prevalence rates of malnutrition, particularly among children, leading to stunted growth and weakened immune systems, leaving them vulnerable to infectious diseases. The nutrition situation is exacerbated by food insecurity in many parts of the country.

Vaccination rates, another vital health indicator, provide insights into the immunization coverage of the population against various diseases. Despite significant strides made in polio eradication, Pakistan remains one of the last polio-endemic countries in the world. Routine immunization coverage for diseases such as measles, diphtheria, and pertussis also need substantial improvement.

Access to safe drinking water and sanitation is another critical health indicator that affects disease prevalence. While there has been progress, a substantial part of the population, particularly in rural areas, still lacks access to clean water and sanitation facilities.

Overall, these health indicators and outcomes portray a healthcare system under significant strain, dealing with a broad spectrum of health challenges from infectious diseases and poor sanitation to increasing non-communicable diseases. This situation calls for comprehensive and context-specific interventions that address not only healthcare provision but also underlying social determinants of health.

Challenges in the Healthcare System

Pakistan's healthcare system faces several significant challenges that hinder its ability to provide accessible, quality care to all citizens. These challenges are manifold and interconnected, encompassing issues of access, quality, financial constraints, and health disparities.

Access to healthcare remains a key challenge, particularly for rural and impoverished populations. Despite improvements over the years, a substantial portion of the population still lacks access to basic healthcare services. The distribution of healthcare facilities is skewed towards urban areas, leaving rural populations underserved. Moreover, even when healthcare facilities are physically accessible, cultural barriers, such as gender norms, may prevent certain populations, like women, from seeking care.

The quality of care is another significant challenge. Inconsistencies in the quality of healthcare services, from diagnostic accuracy to patient management, plague the healthcare system. Contributing factors include outdated equipment, shortages of essential drugs, inadequate supervision, and the lack of standardized treatment protocols.

Financial constraints further exacerbate healthcare challenges in Pakistan. Public healthcare facilities, which are supposed to provide free or affordable care, often suffer from insufficient funding, leading to shortages of essential resources. On the other hand, private healthcare, which generally offers better-quality care, is unaffordable for many. This situation is aggravated by the lack of widespread health insurance coverage, forcing many families into out-of-pocket payments that can lead to catastrophic health expenditures.

Health disparities, both geographical and socio-economic, represent another significant challenge. Health outcomes and access to care vary considerably across provinces, urban and rural areas, and different socio-economic groups. This inequality is reflected in disparate health indicators such as life expectancy, infant and maternal mortality rates, and disease prevalence.

Furthermore, the healthcare system faces challenges from frequent outbreaks of infectious diseases, the growing burden of non-communicable diseases, and environmental health risks, which test its capacity and resilience.

Addressing these challenges requires a comprehensive, multi-sectoral approach that considers the intricate interplay of economic, social, and environmental determinants of health. As such, the roadmap for improving Pakistan's healthcare system involves not only health sector reforms but also broader socio-economic development.

Conclusion

In conclusion, the current state of Pakistan's healthcare system is marked by significant challenges spanning access to care, quality of services, financial constraints, and health disparities. Though progress has been made over the years, a concerted, multi-sectoral effort is needed to surmount these challenges and ensure equitable, quality healthcare for all Pakistanis. The discussions in this chapter underscore the urgent need for robust healthcare reforms aligned with broader socio-economic development.

7.2 CHALLENGES AND TRIUMPHS IN PUBLIC HEALTH

Public health, a critical aspect of any nation's well-being, encompasses a vast field concerned with protecting and improving the health of people and their communities. It involves efforts to prevent health problems before they occur, focusing on the health of entire populations rather than individuals. For a country like Pakistan, with its diverse and substantial population, understanding and addressing public health issues is of paramount importance. This chapter aims to provide a comprehensive overview of the public health landscape in Pakistan, dissecting the major challenges it faces, such as infectious diseases, malnutrition, and poor sanitation, as well as celebrating the triumphs achieved in recent years. As we delve into these aspects, we shall elucidate the intricate interplay between these issues, and their profound impact on the health and well-being of Pakistan's populace, thereby underlining the crucial role of public health in shaping the nation's future.

Understanding Public Health Challenges

Pakistan, with its vast and diverse population, faces a multitude of public health challenges that impede its progress towards achieving robust health outcomes. To comprehend these challenges, we need to delve into several key issues that have persisted over the years.

Firstly, infectious diseases, including tuberculosis, hepatitis, and polio, continue to pose significant health threats. Despite concerted efforts to eradicate them, these diseases still persist, primarily due to inadequate vaccination coverage, poor public awareness, and in the case of polio, security issues that hamper vaccination campaigns. In the case of COVID-19, for instance, the global pandemic has further exposed and exacerbated the weaknesses in Pakistan's healthcare system.

Secondly, malnutrition, especially among children and women, is another critical public health concern. Malnourished children not only face immediate health risks but are also more likely to encounter developmental issues that could affect their cognitive abilities, educational attainment, and future economic productivity. Pregnant women suffering from malnutrition face increased risks during childbirth, which also affects the health of newborns, perpetuating a cycle of poor health.

Another crucial challenge lies in the area of sanitation and hygiene. A significant portion of Pakistan's population still lacks access to clean drinking water and proper sanitation facilities. This leads to the spread of waterborne diseases and poses severe health risks, especially for children.

Lastly, lack of health education contributes significantly to these public health challenges. Many people in Pakistan lack basic knowledge about disease prevention, nutrition, and the importance of hygiene. This gap in health literacy hinders the effective use of health services and contributes to the persistence of preventable diseases.

Addressing these public health challenges requires a comprehensive and integrated approach, involving not only the health sector but also education, infrastructure, and other relevant sectors. Additionally, it requires the active participation of communities, which are at the frontlines of these public health challenges.

Case Studies of Major Public Health Challenges

Infectious Diseases

Pakistan grapples with a significant burden of infectious diseases, which pose a considerable threat to public health. Among these, malaria, dengue, tuberculosis, and more recently, COVID-19, are of paramount concern.

Malaria and dengue are widespread in several regions of Pakistan, particularly during the monsoon season, with the incidence often correlated with socioeconomic factors and lack of effective vector control measures. Tuberculosis is another disease that has stubbornly persisted, partly due to ineffective detection and treatment strategies and partly due to the stigma associated with the disease that prevents patients from seeking timely medical help.

The COVID-19 pandemic has further exposed the vulnerabilities in Pakistan's healthcare system. Despite the implementation of nationwide lockdowns and other measures, the country has faced difficulties in controlling the spread of the virus, owing to several factors such as population density, inadequate healthcare infrastructure, and misinformation.

Malnutrition

Malnutrition remains a pervasive public health challenge in Pakistan, particularly among women and children. According to the National Nutrition Survey 2018, nearly 40% of children under five years are stunted, and 18% are severely malnourished. High rates of maternal malnutrition also contribute to these distressing statistics, with almost half of all pregnant women in Pakistan being anaemic.

The reasons for widespread malnutrition are multifaceted. Factors such as food insecurity, inadequate dietary diversity, lack of knowledge about nutritious food, and inadequate breastfeeding and complementary feeding practices contribute to this public health crisis. The long-term impacts of malnutrition are severe, including impaired cognitive development, reduced immunity, and increased susceptibility to diseases.

Poor Sanitation

Poor sanitation and inadequate access to clean water remain significant challenges in Pakistan, particularly in rural areas. According to UNICEF, only 63% of the population in Pakistan has access to a sanitation facility that is not shared with other households. The lack of proper sanitation facilities and clean water sources contributes significantly to the spread of waterborne diseases, such as diarrhoea and typhoid, which are significant causes of child mortality in Pakistan.

The issue of poor sanitation is not merely a health concern; it is a socioeconomic challenge. It is a reflection of the inequality in resource allocation and the insufficient emphasis on public health in urban planning. Women and girls, in particular, face additional safety and dignity-related issues due to inadequate sanitation facilities. Improving sanitation, therefore, is critical not only for public health but also for social equity and dignity.

Triumphs in Public Health

Despite the significant challenges, Pakistan has also achieved noteworthy triumphs in public health over the years, brought about by concerted efforts, policies, and interventions at both national and international levels.

One of the most significant public health achievements in Pakistan is the progress made in the fight against polio. The country was once considered one of the last strongholds of polio, with hundreds of cases reported each year. However, through nationwide vaccination campaigns, stringent surveillance, and public health education initiatives, Pakistan has made considerable progress towards polio eradication. The number of polio cases has dropped drastically, from 306 in 2014 to just 5 as of June 2023. The fight against polio has been a testament to what can be achieved with sustained effort, resources, and commitment.

Another area where Pakistan has shown commendable progress is in improving maternal and child health. Various programs, often in collaboration with international partners, have been instrumental in enhancing antenatal care, promoting institutional deliveries, and improving immunization coverage. For instance, the Lady Health Workers (LHW) program, launched in 1994, has played a pivotal role in enhancing access to primary healthcare services, particularly for women and children in rural areas. Today, the program employs more than 100,000 female health workers who provide essential health services to millions of people across the country.

Sanitation and hygiene have also seen some improvement, albeit gradual. The government, in collaboration with organizations like UNICEF and the World Bank, has initiated several projects to improve access to clean water and sanitation facilities. The 'Clean Green Pakistan Movement' launched by the government aims to tackle environmental and sanitation issues head-on, promoting behaviours such as handwashing, waste management, and toilet usage.

Sehat Insaf Card

One of Imran Khan's key health reforms as Prime Minister was the introduction of the Sehat Insaf Card, a universal health insurance program that provides free medical treatment to all Pakistanis. The Sehat Insaf Card has been praised for making healthcare more accessible and affordable for millions of Pakistanis.

Khan's government also launched a number of other health initiatives, including increasing the health budget, hiring more doctors and nurses, building new hospitals and clinics. Moreover, his government dealt with the COVID-19 epidemic, while increasing vaccination rates and reducing child mortality.

These triumphs underscore the transformative power of well-planned, sustained public health interventions. Despite the remaining challenges, these successes provide valuable lessons for tackling other public health issues in Pakistan and demonstrate the potential for even greater improvements in the future.

Conclusion

The public health landscape in Pakistan, characterized by numerous challenges and significant triumphs, highlights the critical role of health in the nation's development. The significant issues surrounding infectious diseases, malnutrition, and poor sanitation demand attention and investment, not just for the well-being of individuals, but for the overall socioeconomic prosperity of the country. However, the noteworthy progress made in areas such as polio eradication, maternal and child health, and improved sanitation demonstrates the power of strategic, sustained public health interventions.

The lessons gleaned from these triumphs should inform future efforts and policies, particularly the necessity for cross-sector collaboration, inclusive interventions, and sustained commitment. It is only by addressing these public health challenges and building on the triumphs that Pakistan can ensure better health outcomes for its people, an indispensable ingredient for a prosperous future. Every step taken towards this goal is a step towards a healthier, stronger nation.

8. ENVIRONMENTAL ISSUES

8.1 THE EMERGING ENVIRONMENTAL CRISIS

In an era characterized by rapid technological advances and industrial growth, the devastating effects of an emerging environmental crisis have become increasingly conspicuous. The environmental crisis encapsulates a multitude of problems - from climate change and biodiversity loss to deforestation, pollution, and water scarcity, all posing profound threats to our planet. Particularly in Pakistan, a country where economy and livelihoods are deeply intertwined with natural resources, these challenges bear far-reaching implications. As a developing nation with a booming population, Pakistan is on the front lines of this crisis. It grapples with escalating environmental issues that not only undermine its economic growth and social development but also pose substantial risks to human health, equality, and overall quality of life. In light of these dire circumstances, understanding Pakistan's emerging environmental crisis and its subsequent repercussions becomes a matter of paramount importance. This chapter aims to delve into these critical concerns, shedding light on their causes, effects, and potential solutions.

Understanding the Environmental Crisis

At the heart of the environmental crisis is a wide range of interconnected problems, each contributing to the deterioration of our planet's health. The first and perhaps the most alarming of these is climate change, induced by the rampant release of greenhouse gases into the atmosphere. Fueled by industrial activities, deforestation, and excessive use of fossil fuels, climate change manifests in rising global temperatures, erratic weather patterns, and sea-level rise. Particularly in Pakistan, the impacts are felt through frequent heatwaves, shifting monsoon patterns, and glacial melts leading to floods.

Another significant component of the environmental crisis is the loss of biodiversity. This pertains to the alarming rate at which species of plants and animals are becoming extinct, primarily due to habitat destruction, climate change, pollution, and overexploitation. Biodiversity loss disrupts ecosystems, making them less resilient, impacting everything from food production to disease control.

Pollution, another facet of the environmental crisis, refers to the introduction of harmful materials into the environment. It can take multiple forms: air, water, and soil pollution, each carrying its unique set of detrimental effects. In Pakistan, air pollution caused by vehicle emissions, industrial discharge, and crop burning is a serious concern, leading to severe health issues and a decrease in life expectancy.

Deforestation, the clearing of forest lands usually for agriculture, urbanization, or logging, is another crucial element of the crisis. It not only contributes to climate change by increasing the level of carbon dioxide in the atmosphere but also leads to soil erosion, disruption of water cycles, and loss of biodiversity.

Lastly, water scarcity, caused by overuse and pollution of water resources, along with climate change-induced changes in rainfall patterns, poses a severe threat, especially in Pakistan, where a significant portion of the population and agriculture relies on the Indus River system.

In summary, the environmental crisis is a multifaceted issue, encompassing a range of deeply interconnected challenges that demand urgent attention and action.

Pakistan's Specific Challenges

Climate Change and Its Impacts

Climate change poses a formidable challenge to Pakistan. Situated at the intersection of three of the world's most significant mountain ranges - the Himalayas, the Karakoram, and the Hindu Kush, Pakistan is especially vulnerable to glacial melt. This has led to an increase in flood events, causing widespread devastation. The country's reliance on agriculture also leaves it exposed to the adverse effects of shifting monsoon patterns and temperature rises that can disrupt crop growth. Moreover, increasing instances of heatwaves, particularly in urban centers like Karachi, result in numerous fatalities annually. Thus, climate change has a pervasive impact on Pakistan's natural environment and its socio-economic conditions.

Air and Water Pollution

Air and water pollution are escalating crises in Pakistan. High levels of particulate matter in many Pakistani cities, primarily due to vehicle emissions, industrial output, and crop burning, lead to severe air quality deterioration, resulting in health complications and premature deaths. Water pollution, fueled by the unregulated disposal of industrial waste and inadequate sanitation services, has rendered many water bodies unfit for consumption. Diseases caused by contaminated water like cholera, diarrhoea, and typhoid are prevalent, affecting particularly the underserved communities.

Deforestation and Biodiversity Loss

Pakistan's forests are under threat from deforestation due to urban expansion, agriculture, logging, and energy projects. The loss of forest cover contributes to climate change, destabilizes ecosystems, and threatens the diverse flora and fauna native to these regions. Mangrove forests in the Indus Delta, home to a unique ecosystem, have witnessed significant depletion, disrupting the livelihoods of local communities and endangering various species. Similarly, northern Pakistan's rich biodiversity is at risk due to habitat destruction and illegal wildlife trade.

Water Scarcity

Water scarcity is a grave issue in Pakistan. The country's primary water source, the Indus River, is under pressure due to overuse, pollution, and the effects of climate change. Despite being an agrarian economy that relies heavily on irrigation, inefficient water use, and inadequate infrastructure contribute to water wastage. Rapid urbanization and population growth further increase demand, straining the already limited water resources. The scarcity is particularly severe in arid regions of Balochistan and Tharparkar, where communities often struggle for access to clean water. If unchecked, water scarcity could trigger a crisis of food security, health, and socio-economic development in the country.

Consequences of the Crisis

The environmental crisis Pakistan faces has far-reaching implications for the country's socio-economic landscape, public health, and its ambitions towards sustainable development. These consequences are already visible and will likely amplify if not addressed timely and effectively.

Socio-economically, the environmental crisis has a disproportionate impact on vulnerable communities. Climate change-induced weather anomalies, such as floods and droughts, can wipe out agricultural yields, upon which a substantial proportion of Pakistan's rural population depends. Simultaneously, deforestation and biodiversity loss disrupt ecosystem services, affecting livelihoods linked to forestry and fisheries. Furthermore, water scarcity can lead to conflicts over resources and migration as people are forced to move in search of water.

In terms of health, the environmental crisis poses a severe threat. Poor air quality, primarily in urban areas, leads to an increase in respiratory diseases, cardiovascular conditions, and premature deaths. Water pollution, resulting from industrial effluents and lack of adequate sanitation, increases the incidence of waterborne diseases.

From a developmental perspective, the environmental crisis could hamper Pakistan's progress towards its Sustainable Development Goals (SDGs). For example, SDG 13 calls for urgent action to combat climate change and its impacts, which Pakistan is currently struggling with. Similarly, SDG 15, which emphasizes terrestrial ecosystems' protection, is challenged by deforestation and biodiversity loss.

Lastly, Pakistan's environmental crisis also has global implications. As one of the country's most vulnerable to climate change, the environmental challenges it faces underscore the need for international cooperation in mitigating climate change and its impacts. Therefore, Pakistan's environmental crisis not only threatens its internal stability and development but also holds importance in the global fight against climate change.

Conclusion

In conclusion, Pakistan faces an emerging environmental crisis that manifests in various forms: climate change, air and water pollution, deforestation, biodiversity loss, and water scarcity. These challenges have profound implications for the socio-economic landscape, health, and sustainable development goals of the country. The crisis threatens livelihoods, exacerbates health problems, and impedes progress towards achieving sustainable development. Moreover, these challenges also underline Pakistan's role in the global fight against climate change. The country's specific vulnerability to the impacts of climate change highlights the need for both local and global action. In the face of this escalating crisis, there is an urgent need for effective solutions, strategies, and policies that can address these environmental challenges. The forthcoming discussion will delve into potential measures that Pakistan can adopt to mitigate the effects of this crisis and build a more sustainable and resilient future.

8.2 PAKISTAN'S ROLE IN GLOBAL CLIMATE CHANGE

Global climate change is an existential crisis that threatens all nations and necessitates immediate collective action. Despite varying contributions to the problem, every country bears the consequences, some more severely than others. Pakistan, situated in a vulnerable region, exemplifies this reality. Its contribution to the world's total greenhouse gas emissions is a meagre 0.8%, but it ranks 5th on the Global Climate Risk Index, making it one of the country's most susceptible to climate change impacts. This paradox underlines the urgency for Pakistan to both mitigate its emissions and adapt to the inevitable changes, asserting a vital role in the global climate conversation.

Pakistan's Contribution to Global Greenhouse Gas Emissions

Pakistan, with its growing population and industrial development, contributes to global greenhouse gas emissions, albeit to a lesser extent compared to major emitters. A closer look at its emissions profile reveals the major sources of these emissions.

Energy production, primarily fueled by coal, oil, and natural gas, is the largest contributor, accounting for approximately 50% of Pakistan's total emissions. Power plants, residential energy use, and transport are the primary culprits here. Pakistan's burgeoning industrial sector also contributes significantly, emitting greenhouse gases through manufacturing processes and the burning of fossil fuels.

Agriculture, a crucial sector of Pakistan's economy, is another notable contributor, accounting for nearly 39% of the country's total emissions. Livestock farming, rice production, and the application of synthetic fertilizers release substantial quantities of methane and nitrous oxide, potent greenhouse gases.

Finally, deforestation and land-use changes further amplify Pakistan's emissions profile. Pakistan's forests, which act as carbon sinks, are rapidly diminishing due to urbanization, agriculture, and illegal logging, resulting in increased carbon dioxide levels in the atmosphere.

As of 2020, Pakistan's total greenhouse gas emissions were estimated to be around 405 million tons of carbon dioxide equivalent, reflecting its contribution to the global climate crisis.

Impacts of Climate Change on Pakistan

Climate change has profound implications for Pakistan, a country whose economy and population are heavily dependent on its natural resources. The impacts range from disrupted weather patterns and agricultural output to dwindling water resources and heightened vulnerability to natural disasters.

Pakistan's weather patterns have become increasingly erratic due to climate change, with alternating periods of extreme heat and cold, and unpredictable rainfall. These shifts have serious consequences for agriculture, a sector that employs almost 40% of the nation's workforce and contributes to a significant portion of the GDP. Changes in temperature and rainfall patterns can lead to reduced crop yields and livestock productivity, thereby threatening food security and rural livelihoods.

Moreover, climate change is exacerbating Pakistan's water crisis.

Rising temperatures have led to rapid glacial melt in the Himalayas, the source of most of Pakistan's freshwater. While this initially increases water flow, in the long term, it risks drying up these critical water sources. This is alarming for a country where agriculture, which relies heavily on irrigation, is a mainstay of the economy.

Pakistan is also at the mercy of intensified natural disasters, such as floods and droughts. The increased frequency and intensity of these events, driven by climate change, wreak havoc on communities, causing loss of lives, displacing populations, and inflicting extensive damage to infrastructure and the economy. For instance, the devastating floods of 2010, exacerbated by climate change, affected 20 million people, and caused about $10 billion in damages.

Climate change also poses significant health risks in Pakistan, from heat-related illnesses and diseases spread by contaminated water to vector-borne diseases like malaria and dengue, which are becoming more widespread with changing climatic conditions.

The impacts of climate change on Pakistan are severe and far-reaching, demanding urgent attention and action to mitigate the effects and adapt to a changing climate.

Pakistan's Actions to Address Climate Change

Recognizing the growing threat of climate change, Pakistan has taken several important steps to mitigate its impacts and adapt to new realities. The country's actions span from implementing national policies to actively participating in international climate negotiations.

One notable initiative is the Billion Tree Tsunami project, launched in 2014, aimed at combating deforestation and offsetting carbon emissions. This successful project has not only helped sequester carbon but also created job opportunities and protected biodiversity. It has since been expanded into a "Ten Billion Tree Tsunami" program, reflecting Pakistan's commitment to using nature-based solutions to address climate change.

In terms of policy, the National Climate Change Policy, developed in 2012, provides a comprehensive framework to address climate issues. It lays out strategies for climate change mitigation and adaptation, spanning various sectors such as water, agriculture, and energy. However, translating this policy into action remains a challenge due to financial constraints, capacity issues, and the need for coordination across different levels of government and sectors.

PTI government—architects of the billion-tree tsunami project—had also set the goal of increasing the share of renewable energy in the country's energy mix to 30% by 2030. Their term also saw efforts to reduce Pakistan's water scarcity by building the Diamer-Bhasha dam.

At the international level, Pakistan actively participates in climate negotiations under the United Nations Framework Convention on Climate Change (UNFCCC). The country has consistently advocated for the principles of equity and common but differentiated responsibilities, highlighting the need for developed countries to support climate action in developing countries.

Finally, Pakistan faces significant adaptation needs, particularly in agriculture and water management. Initiatives like climate-smart agriculture and improved water conservation measures are being implemented but require greater attention and resources.

In sum, while Pakistan has made strides in addressing climate change, the scale of the challenge requires increased efforts, resources, and international support. Despite its limited contribution to global emissions, the country has shown commitment to being part of the solution.

Pakistan's Role in the Global Fight Against Climate Change

As a developing nation acutely vulnerable to climate change, Pakistan holds a critical position in global climate discussions. Its experiences can serve as an influential narrative for other nations similarly grappling with climate change, underscoring the urgency of this global crisis. Moreover, with its vast potential in renewable energy, especially solar and wind, and sustainable agriculture, Pakistan has the opportunity to contribute to global climate solutions while enhancing its own sustainable development. However, realizing this potential necessitates increased international cooperation, including technology transfer and climate financing. Pakistan's role underlines the interconnected nature of climate change, where actions in one country have ripple effects globally, reinforcing the need for shared responsibility and collective action.

8.3 SOLUTIONS AND STRATEGIES FOR A SUSTAINABLE FUTURE

In an era where environmental crises are escalating, it has become more crucial than ever to develop solutions and strategies for a sustainable future. Sustainability is not just a buzzword; it's a comprehensive approach that nations need to adopt for long-term socio-economic and environmental prosperity. This is particularly relevant for developing countries like Pakistan, which, while grappling with various environmental challenges, also possess the potential to turn the tide towards sustainability. Pakistan's unique geographical position, natural resources, and youthful population can be significant assets if harnessed correctly. This chapter will delve into an array of sustainable strategies suitable for Pakistan, exploring the practicality and potential impact of each. From renewable energy and sustainable agriculture to waste management and education, we will examine how these solutions can be integrated into Pakistan's national fabric to ensure a prosperous and sustainable future.

The Concept of Sustainability

Sustainability is a holistic concept that transcends beyond mere environmental considerations. It's a principle based on the harmony between human activities and the natural world, with an eye on the well-being of future generations. The United Nations' Brundtland Report (1987) famously defines sustainable development as development that "meets the needs of the present without compromising the ability of future generations to meet their own needs."

Fundamentally, sustainability rests on three pillars: economic, social, and environmental, often represented as a Venn diagram showing areas of overlap. These pillars underline that sustainability is not a single-track pursuit, but rather a balanced interplay of multiple components.

The economic pillar emphasizes the need for economic growth and stability. It includes elements such as job creation, economic diversification, technological innovation, and responsible consumption. In a sustainable economic model, growth is driven in ways that positively impact society and the environment, without depleting resources for future generations.

The social pillar is centered on improving the quality of life for all individuals in a society. This includes issues like human rights, health and well-being, education, social justice, gender equality, cultural diversity, and political participation. Sustainable societies are those that are inclusive, equitable, and foster strong community ties.

The environmental pillar, perhaps the most widely recognized, emphasizes the preservation and enhancement of the natural world. It focuses on reducing pollution, promoting biodiversity, conserving natural resources, and shifting towards renewable sources of energy.

In order to achieve true sustainability, it is vital to balance these three pillars. They are interconnected and interdependent; neglecting one can led to the collapse of the whole structure. For example, economic growth at the expense of environmental degradation or social inequality can lead to long-term damage and instability. Therefore, the challenge lies in devising strategies that synergize these three pillars to pave the way towards a sustainable future.

Solutions for a Sustainable Future

Renewable Energy

Transitioning to renewable energy is a crucial strategy for a sustainable future. Pakistan has immense potential for renewable energy sources like solar and wind energy. The country's geographic location gives it abundant sunlight, making it ideally suited for solar power generation. Similarly, regions like Sindh and Balochistan have high wind speeds, ideal for wind energy generation. Harnessing these resources could significantly reduce dependence on fossil fuels, curtail greenhouse gas emissions, and provide a sustainable solution to Pakistan's energy crisis. Government incentives and policies promoting renewable energy infrastructure, alongside private sector investment, are necessary for this transition.

Sustainable Agriculture

Sustainable agriculture plays a pivotal role in balancing food security and environmental protection. In Pakistan, water conservation techniques like drip irrigation and sprinkler systems can optimize water use, vital in a water-stressed country. Organic farming, avoiding harmful pesticides and fertilizers, can improve soil health and biodiversity. Agroforestry, integrating trees into farmlands, can enhance productivity and resilience while contributing to carbon sequestration. Government policies and programs can encourage such practices, and farmer education can expedite their adoption.

Waste Management

Effective waste management is vital for a sustainable future. In Pakistan, strategies like recycling, composting, and waste-to-energy projects can mitigate pollution and conserve resources. For example, organic waste can be composted to enrich soils, while inorganic waste can be recycled or transformed into energy. Community-led initiatives, public-private partnerships, and policies enforcing waste segregation can foster these practices.

Conservation and Restoration of Ecosystems

Conserving and restoring ecosystems like forests, wetlands, and grasslands is crucial for mitigating climate change and preserving biodiversity. These ecosystems act as carbon sinks, absorbing CO_2 emissions. In Pakistan, initiatives like the Billion Tree Tsunami aim to restore deforested areas and combat climate change. Protecting natural habitats from encroachment and overexploitation is equally essential to maintain biodiversity. A combined approach of strict enforcement of environmental regulations, protected area expansion, and community participation in conservation can ensure the success of these efforts.

Education and Awareness

Education and public awareness are instrumental in promoting sustainability. In Pakistan, integrating environmental education into school curricula can build an understanding of sustainable practices from a young age. Public awareness campaigns about issues like water conservation, waste segregation, and energy efficiency can change behaviours and increase public demand for sustainable policies. Moreover, capacity building programs can equip policymakers, business leaders, and community members with the knowledge and skills needed to drive sustainable development. Thus, education serves as a foundation for fostering a society committed to sustainability.

Implementing Sustainable Strategies

Implementing sustainable strategies in Pakistan involves a myriad of challenges, yet also presents significant opportunities.

One major challenge is the initial financial investment required for initiatives such as renewable energy infrastructure, sustainable farming systems, or waste management facilities. These costs can be prohibitive, particularly for a developing economy. Moreover, the transition towards sustainability might face resistance from established industries that perceive it as a threat to their interests.

However, these challenges are not insurmountable. International cooperation can play a vital role in overcoming financial constraints. Partnerships with developed countries and international organizations can provide necessary funds, technological transfer, and capacity-building programs. For instance, the Green Climate Fund, set up under the UNFCCC, supports developing countries in their response to climate change.

Technological innovation also plays a crucial role. From developing more efficient solar panels to devising water-saving irrigation systems, innovation can lower costs and improve effectiveness of sustainable strategies. Pakistan's burgeoning tech industry could become a driving force in this regard.

Government policies are central to implementing sustainable strategies. Regulations that incentivize renewable energy, protect natural resources, and promote sustainable practices can create an enabling environment. The government can also invest in infrastructure, research, and education to support sustainable development.

Lastly, the role of community participation cannot be overstated. Sustainable strategies are most effective when they are rooted in the local context and engage the local population. Communities can play a key role in implementing and maintaining projects, and their engagement ensures that the benefits of sustainability are widely shared. Hence, a bottom-up approach can complement top-down policies.

In conclusion, while implementing sustainable strategies in Pakistan involves challenges, the opportunities they present for a resilient and prosperous future make them worth pursuing.

Conclusion

In conclusion, achieving a sustainable future in Pakistan involves tackling a broad spectrum of issues, from renewable energy adoption to sustainable agriculture, waste management, ecosystem conservation, and education. Despite challenges, successful implementation of sustainable strategies, aided by technological innovation, governmental support, and international cooperation, is both a critical and attainable goal for a prosperous Pakistan.

9. GENDER AND SOCIAL INEQUALITY

9.1 UNDERSTANDING SOCIAL STRATIFICATION IN PAKISTAN

Social stratification is a fundamental concept in sociology, referring to the hierarchical arrangement of individuals within a society, where societal roles and access to resources are distributed unevenly. These divisions are typically based on class, caste, race, ethnicity, and gender. Stratification shapes various aspects of people's lives, including their opportunities, rights, and access to vital resources. In the context of Pakistan, a country characterized by a rich ethnic diversity and a complex social tapestry, social stratification manifests in intricate ways, reflecting the country's unique historical, cultural, and economic dimensions. This chapter will delve into the nature of social stratification in Pakistan, discussing its origins, manifestations, and implications. We will explore economic disparities, ethnic and linguistic divisions, gender inequalities, and the urban-rural divide, providing a comprehensive view of the social landscape in Pakistan.

Concept of Social Stratification

Social stratification is the process by which societies categorize people into different ranks or statuses based on various attributes such as wealth, occupation, education, ethnicity, and gender. This stratification creates an ordered system of social hierarchy that significantly influences individuals' life chances, access to resources, and power.

In the context of class stratification, individuals and groups are divided into 'upper,' 'middle,' and 'lower' classes. Class typically refers to economic position and is often determined by income, wealth, and occupation. In Pakistan, the social class system is intricately tied to economic disparities. For instance, the upper class, consisting of wealthy businesspeople, landlords, and high-ranking professionals, often have greater access to resources such as high-quality education, healthcare, and social networks, compared to the middle and lower classes.

Caste-based stratification, although officially abolished, still exists in many parts of Pakistan, particularly in rural areas. It is a form of social stratification that categorizes people into hereditary groups with a social hierarchy. The caste system in Pakistan is less rigid than in some other South Asian countries but nonetheless significantly influences individuals' social standing, marriage prospects, and occupations.

Ethnic stratification is another key dimension, given Pakistan's diverse ethnic composition, including Punjabis, Sindhis, Baloch, Pashtuns, and others. Each ethnic group has distinct cultural practices, languages, and social norms, which often contribute to a sense of group identity and solidarity. However, the differential treatment of various ethnic groups can often lead to social inequalities and tensions.

Lastly, gender stratification is a universal phenomenon where societies assign different roles, responsibilities, and social value to individuals based on their sex. In Pakistan, patriarchal norms and traditional gender roles often result in women having less access to resources, fewer opportunities, and lower status than men. Gender stratification intersects with other forms of stratification, further compounding the inequality experienced by women from lower classes, castes, or marginalized ethnic groups.

These different dimensions of social stratification often intersect, creating a complex web of social inequality in Pakistan. An understanding of these dynamics is crucial for developing policies and interventions aimed at promoting social equality and justice.

Social Stratification in Pakistan

Economic Class

Pakistan's economic landscape is marked by significant income inequalities, which give rise to distinct class stratifications. The wealthy elite, consisting of industrialists, landowners, and high-ranking professionals, make up a small portion of the population, yet they control a substantial portion of the country's wealth. This wealth disparity is rooted in historical processes, such as colonial land ownership systems, and contemporary economic policies favouring certain sectors over others.

At the other end of the spectrum, the lower class, characterized by low income and precarious work conditions, makes up a significant portion of the population. This class includes daily wage laborers, small-scale farmers, and the urban poor. The middle class, though growing, often faces economic instability due to inflation and job insecurity. The economic disparities among these classes are further accentuated by unequal access to quality education, healthcare, and other social services.

Ethnicity and Language

Ethnic and linguistic diversity in Pakistan significantly contribute to the social stratification. The main ethnic groups, including Punjabis, Sindhis, Pashtuns, Baloch, and Muhajirs, each have unique cultural practices, languages, and historical experiences. This diversity, while enriching the cultural fabric of the nation, has also resulted in varying degrees of socio-economic development, political representation, and access to resources among different ethnic groups.

For instance, Punjabis, being the majority ethnic group, have had a historically dominant position in politics and the military, which often leads to resentment from other ethnic groups. Similarly, the Sindhi language in education and administration in Sindh province creates a linguistic hierarchy that disadvantages Urdu and other language speakers. These ethnic and linguistic disparities often result in social inequalities and can lead to intergroup conflicts.

Gender

Gender is a pivotal dimension of social stratification in Pakistan. Despite making up half the population, women face considerable barriers in accessing education, economic opportunities, and political representation. Traditional patriarchal norms often confine women to domestic roles, limiting their participation in public life. Furthermore, harmful practices such as early marriage and honour crimes continue to affect women's social standing and personal freedoms.

Women's experiences of gender inequality are not monolithic and intersect with class, ethnicity, and urban-rural divide. For instance, rural women, particularly those from marginalized ethnic and lower economic classes, often bear the brunt of gender, class, and ethnic inequalities. The empowerment of women and the dismantling of patriarchal structures are crucial for a more equal and inclusive society.

Urban vs Rural

The urban-rural divide is another key facet of social stratification in Pakistan. Urban areas, particularly major cities like Karachi, Lahore, and Islamabad, are seen as centers of economic opportunities, education, and healthcare facilities. However, rapid urbanization and population growth often lead to overcrowding, inequality, and strain on urban infrastructure.

On the other hand, rural areas, where the majority of the

population resides, often face a lack of basic amenities, including clean drinking water, electricity, quality education, and healthcare. The rural economy, heavily reliant on agriculture, is vulnerable to market fluctuations and climate change. Additionally, rural areas often adhere more strictly to traditional social hierarchies based on class, caste, and gender, further compounding social inequalities.

The urban-rural divide reflects a broader pattern of unequal development and resource allocation, underlining the need for balanced regional development and urban planning policies.

Consequences of Social Stratification

Social stratification in Pakistan, as in any society, has far-reaching consequences that ripple through multiple aspects of social life and individual experiences.

Firstly, social stratification significantly impacts social mobility. The circumstances of one's birth, including class, gender, and ethnicity, can significantly determine their life chances and opportunities. For instance, a child born in a poor rural family will likely face more hurdles in accessing quality education, decent employment, and healthcare compared to their urban, middle-class counterpart. This limitation on social mobility perpetuates a cycle of poverty and inequality across generations.

Access to resources and opportunities is also heavily influenced by social stratification. The economic elite, for example, have greater access to capital, quality education, and influential social networks. On the other hand, the lower economic classes often struggle to meet their basic needs. Similarly, gender, ethnic, and urban-rural disparities manifest in unequal access to resources like healthcare, clean water, and political representation.

Stratification also has profound implications for social cohesion. Deep-seated social inequalities can lead to feelings of marginalization and resentment among disadvantaged groups, contributing to social tensions and conflicts. For instance, ethnic and linguistic disparities in Pakistan have led to instances of civil unrest and demand for greater autonomy by ethnic minorities. Similarly, gender inequalities can foster a culture of discrimination and violence against women.

Finally, social stratification can contribute to societal conflict. Economic inequality can result in class conflicts, while ethnic and linguistic disparities can stoke intergroup tensions. Gender inequality, on the other hand, can result in patriarchal violence and resistance against gender justice movements.

Thus, addressing social stratification is critical for creating a more just and peaceful society. It requires comprehensive social policies that prioritize equitable resource distribution, affirmative action for disadvantaged groups, and a commitment to social justice.

Conclusion

In conclusion, social stratification in Pakistan is a complex and deeply entrenched phenomenon that shapes the fabric of society. This system of stratification, rooted in economic class, ethnicity, language, gender, and the urban-rural divide, determines access to resources, opportunities, and power. It dictates life outcomes, reinforcing cycles of poverty and privilege, often perpetuating these disparities across generations. The impact of such stratification extends beyond individual lives; it affects social cohesion and can even incite societal conflict. As such, understanding social stratification is crucial to comprehending the social dynamics of Pakistan and devising effective policies to promote equality and social justice. The quest for a more egalitarian Pakistan necessitates an unwavering commitment to dismantling these hierarchical structures and nurturing a society where every individual, regardless of their social status at birth, can realize their full potential.

9.2 THE STATE OF GENDER EQUALITY AND HUMAN RIGHTS

Gender equality and human rights are universally recognized principles, key to ensuring dignity, freedom, and equality for every individual, regardless of their gender, race, religion, or nationality. They underpin every aspect of a fair and functioning society and play a pivotal role in promoting peace, democracy, and sustainable development. However, their implementation varies greatly across different socio-cultural contexts, making them critical areas of examination in every nation, including Pakistan.

In Pakistan, a country imbued with rich cultural diversity and stringent societal norms, the discourse on gender equality and human rights gains further complexity. The country is at a crossroads, grappling with the challenges of preserving traditional values while embracing the principles of modern, inclusive societies. Gender disparities, biases in societal norms, legal frameworks, and attitudes, coupled with human rights issues such as freedom of speech and rights of minority groups, paint a multifaceted picture of the current state of gender equality and human rights in Pakistan. This essay will delve deeper into these issues, shedding light on the existing landscape, its challenges, and potential pathways towards a more equitable society.

Understanding Gender Equality and Human Rights

Gender equality refers to the state in which access to rights, responsibilities, and opportunities are not affected by the gender of the individual. It involves the equal valuation of the roles of both women and men, considering their rights, responsibilities, and opportunities. Gender equality does not imply that women and men are the same but acknowledges their differences and the fact that these differences - whether biological, gendered, or socially constructed - must not be a basis for discrimination or privilege.

On the other hand, human rights are inherent to every human being, regardless of nationality, sex, ethnic origin, religion, language, or any other status. These rights encompass the rights to life and liberty, freedom from slavery and torture, freedom of opinion and expression, the right to work and education, among many others. Human rights are enshrined in international law, specifically the Universal Declaration of Human Rights (UDHR), which serves as the cornerstone of modern human rights law.

The UDHR and other international frameworks such as the Convention on the Elimination of All Forms of Discrimination against Women (CEDAW) lay out the universal standards for human rights and gender equality. These conventions assert that all human beings are equal and have the right to live free from discrimination and violence, to participate fully in societal affairs, and to enjoy economic, social, cultural, civil, and political rights.

These concepts are deeply interconnected as gender equality is part of the broader human rights agenda. Gender discrimination often leads to violations of human rights, and therefore, the fight for human rights incorporates the struggle for gender equality. By ensuring human rights, we pave the way for gender equality and vice versa. To realize these twin goals, it is critical to understand the social, cultural, economic, and political structures that create and perpetuate inequalities. This understanding can guide appropriate strategies to challenge and change these structures towards more equitable societies.

Gender Equality in Pakistan

Women's Participation in Public and Economic Life

Despite some progress over the years, women in Pakistan

continue to be underrepresented in public and economic life. The gender disparity is quite stark when it comes to labour force participation. Due to cultural norms and patriarchal values, many women are restricted to unpaid work within the household. Those who do engage in paid labour are often confined to low-skilled, low-wage jobs with limited access to benefits or job security. Furthermore, women's participation in political life is minimal, both in terms of representation in legislative bodies and active political participation at the grassroots level. Although the government has introduced reserved seats for women in legislative assemblies, their representation remains insufficient and women's voices in policymaking are still marginalized.

Education and Health

In the realms of education and health, gender inequality is apparent in Pakistan. The gender gap in education is one of the highest in the world, with the literacy rate for women significantly lower than for men. A complex web of economic, cultural, and societal barriers prevents girls from accessing and completing education. In health, while maternal mortality rates have declined, access to quality healthcare services remains a concern, particularly for women in rural areas. Nutrition disparities are also notable, with women and girls often suffering from malnutrition due to gender-based food allocation practices in households.

Violence Against Women and Discriminatory Laws

Violence against women in Pakistan is a pervasive issue. It encompasses a range of abuses, from domestic violence and so-called 'honour killings' to forced marriages and sexual harassment. Cultural norms and societal attitudes often perpetuate such violence, making it a largely silent issue. Furthermore, while Pakistan has enacted laws aimed at protecting women's rights, implementation remains a significant challenge. Several laws still have discriminatory provisions, particularly in personal law matters related to marriage, divorce, and inheritance. The patriarchal interpretation of religious laws often exacerbates the discrimination against women. In this context, the struggle for gender equality in Pakistan continues, necessitating structural and societal changes that value and uphold the rights of women.

In 2023, Pakistan saw a rise in violence against women as supporters of Pakistan Tehreek-e-Insaf were picked up and harassed. Reports of sexual harassment of PTI's female workers were dismissed by the then Interior Minister, Rana Sana Ullah, who blamed the workers for trying to create a conspiracy. Multiple human rights organizations have condemned actions of Pakistan's government and military against political workers of Pakistan Tehreek-e-Insaf.

Human Rights in Pakistan

Freedom of Speech and Expression

Freedom of speech and expression in Pakistan faces considerable challenges, despite being enshrined in the country's constitution. Journalists, activists, and critics of the government or military often face threats, harassment, and violence. This climate of fear has resulted in self-censorship by many media outlets, impacting the diversity and openness of public discourse. Moreover, the internet and social media, while offering an alternative platform for free expression, have also been subjected to regulatory controls and censorship. Controversial laws, such as blasphemy laws and certain provisions of cybercrime legislation, have been used to suppress free speech under the guise of protecting religious sentiments or national security.

In 2022, journalist Arshad Shareef was assassinated in Kenya for speaking against Pakistan's military. In the months that followed, prominent journalists were arrested to intimidate them. In 2023, Imran Riaz Khan was picked up and disappeared. Many journalists, me included, were forced to leave Pakistan for our and our family's safety. This was a crackdown on journalism and free speech that Pakistan had not seen even in military dictatorships.

Human Rights and the Legal System

The legal system in Pakistan, while having provisions to protect human rights, often falls short in enforcement. The judiciary has been known to uphold human rights in certain landmark cases, but systemic issues like corruption, lengthy trial processes, and limited access to justice for the poor and marginalized undermine its effectiveness. The use of torture in police custody, the lack of due process in cases related to national security, and the application of the death penalty, including for offenses that do not meet the threshold of 'most serious crimes' as per international law, are significant human rights concerns. Despite these challenges, human rights activists, civil society organizations, and certain progressive legislative changes offer hope for the improvement of human rights in Pakistan.

Challenges and Prospects

Pakistan faces significant hurdles in achieving gender equality and human rights, rooted in societal norms, religious interpretations, and political reluctances. Patriarchal structures hinder women's advancement, and minority rights are often sidelined. Legal protections, although present, lack robust enforcement, resulting in widespread impunity. However, prospects for improvement exist. Grassroots movements, civil society activism, and international pressure are triggering discourse and action. Emerging education and economic empowerment programs are promoting women's participation in society. Meanwhile, legal reforms and judgments have occasionally provided progressive precedents. Achieving substantive equality and human rights is a complex, gradual process, but these signs of progress offer a glimmer of hope.

Conclusion

The chapter outlined the complex landscape of gender equality and human rights in Pakistan. The country's socio-cultural fabric and enforcement mechanisms present challenges. However, the emergence of advocacy movements and progressive initiatives provides hope. Ensuring gender equality and upholding human rights remain integral for Pakistan's inclusive and sustainable development.

9.3 TRIUMPHS AND TRIALS ON THE ROAD TO EQUITY

Equity, a foundational principle for any society striving towards justice and fairness, plays an essential role in shaping the social, economic, and political fabric of a country. In the context of Pakistan, a country marked by deep-seated and complex social hierarchies, the pursuit of equity takes on a particularly compelling urgency. This chapter aims to explore the numerous trials and triumphs experienced by Pakistan on its path towards a more equitable society. The discussion will span a diverse range of topics, including gender, social class, and ethnic disparities, highlighting the significant strides made, while also shedding light on the profound challenges that persist.

Understanding Equity

Equity, in its simplest form, refers to fairness and impartiality, embodying the principle that all individuals should have equal access to opportunities and resources irrespective of their personal characteristics such as gender, race, economic status, or ethnicity. It goes beyond the concept of equality, which calls for equal treatment, to advocate for tailored approaches that address underlying inequalities and help level the playing field.

The importance of equity cannot be overstated. It is intrinsically linked to social cohesion and sustainable development. A society marked by significant inequities breeds resentment and discord, potentially leading to social conflict. On the other hand, an equitable society fosters mutual respect and unity among its members, enhancing social stability and cooperation.

From a development perspective, equity is critical for optimizing the utilization of human potential. An equitable society is one where everyone can contribute to their full capacity, thereby maximizing collective productivity and innovation. It also ensures the fair distribution of development benefits, preventing the concentration of wealth and power in the hands of a few.

In the context of Pakistan, pursuing equity is particularly vital given the nation's diverse social fabric and marked disparities across various social strata. As we navigate through the triumphs and trials on this road to equity, it is imperative to acknowledge that equity is not merely an ideal to aspire to; it's a necessity for a prosperous and harmonious society.

Triumphs Towards Equity in Pakistan

Progress in Gender Equity

Pakistan has made considerable strides towards gender equity, particularly in the legal and institutional framework. The passage of laws against gender-based violence, including the Protection against Harassment of Women at Workplace Act and the Punjab Protection of Women against Violence Act, mark significant milestones. Simultaneously, there have been efforts to increase women's participation in public and economic life. Women now serve in prominent roles across the government, judiciary, and corporate sectors. Moreover, initiatives like the Benazir Income Support Program aim at economically empowering women by providing them with direct cash transfers.

Progress in Social Equity

When it comes to social equity, Pakistan has also witnessed some progress. Policies have been adopted to address the disparities among different social classes, ethnicities, and religious groups. Affirmative action policies, such as quotas for marginalized groups in government jobs and educational institutions, have opened new avenues of opportunity for these communities. Legislation against discrimination, such as the Punjab Fair Representation of Women Act, has been enforced to ensure equal representation.

There has also been a focus on promoting the rights of religious minorities, with the government setting up the National Commission for Minorities to protect their rights and interests. Furthermore, efforts are being made to uplift underprivileged regions, with increased investment in education, health, and infrastructure in areas like Balochistan and rural Sindh. These efforts signify important steps towards a more equitable society.

Moving Forward

Achieving equity in Pakistan is a continuing endeavour requiring persistent efforts, dynamic policy changes, and deep-rooted societal transformation. The government must ensure effective implementation of laws and foster policies that promote equity. Civil society's role is equally crucial in raising awareness and advocating for change. International organizations can assist by providing technical support, facilitating knowledge exchange, and advocating for global standards. The collective action of these stakeholders is critical to address systemic barriers and pave the way for an equitable society.

Conclusion

This chapter explored the complex journey towards equity in Pakistan, highlighting both the triumphs and trials. It underscored the importance of concerted efforts from all segments of society to ensure a fair, inclusive, and equitable Pakistan. While challenges persist, the strides made offer a beacon of hope, underscoring that a more equitable future is not only necessary but also achievable.

10. SECURITY CONCERNS

10.1 INTERNAL SECURITY ISSUES AND TERRORISM

Internal security, a crucial factor in a nation's progress, refers to the actions taken by a state to ensure the safety and protection of its citizens against internal threats. This involves maintaining law and order, thwarting criminal activities, and safeguarding against threats to the nation's unity and integrity. One of the most formidable challenges to internal security worldwide is terrorism, an illicit tactic characterized by violent acts aimed at causing fear and instability.

For Pakistan, a country enriched with a diverse cultural fabric and a complex political history, maintaining internal security while countering terrorism has been an ongoing challenge. Over the years, the country has faced an array of internal security issues ranging from political instability, sectarian violence, to organized crime, all interwoven with the pervasive threat of terrorism. The multifaceted nature of these internal threats not only jeopardizes the safety and wellbeing of citizens, but it also poses significant hurdles to the country's socio-economic development and global standing. This essay explores the intricate landscape of internal security issues and terrorism in Pakistan, providing insights into their roots, manifestations, and potential solutions.

Understanding Internal Security and Terrorism

Internal security involves all measures adopted by a state to protect its citizens, maintain the rule of law, and uphold social harmony within its boundaries. It encapsulates various dimensions including safeguarding against domestic threats such as criminal activity, insurgencies, riots, and other disturbances that can disrupt societal peace and stability. While the precise factors affecting internal security can vary, typically they include political instability, socio-economic disparities, corruption, and weaknesses in law enforcement institutions.

Political instability, marked by frequent changes in government, policy inconsistency, and political violence, can undermine the ability of the state to maintain order and control, thus compromising internal security. Socio-economic disparities, such as high levels of poverty, unemployment, and income inequality, can lead to social unrest, breeding grounds for criminal activity and other threats to internal security. Corruption and weak law enforcement institutions can also undermine security by eroding public trust, impeding the effective enforcement of laws, and facilitating criminal activities.

Terrorism, on the other hand, is characterized as the use or threat of violence, often motivated by ideological, political, or religious extremism, to instil fear, disrupt society, and challenge established order. Terrorism constitutes a major threat to internal security as it seeks to destabilize the state, undermine societal harmony, and cause widespread fear and damage.

The roots of terrorism can be complex and multifaceted, often intertwining with socio-political conditions. Ideological extremism, whether religious, political, or ethno-nationalist in nature, often serves as a motivating force for terrorism, providing the ideological justification for violent acts. Political conflicts, whether internal or with neighbouring countries, can give rise to, or exacerbate, terrorism, especially if they involve grievances that are not addressed through peaceful means. Social inequalities, including lack of access to quality education, economic opportunities, and political marginalization, can also contribute to the radicalization and recruitment of individuals into terrorist groups. In the context of Pakistan, these factors and more contribute to both internal security issues and the persistence of terrorism.

Internal Security Issues in Pakistan

Political and Sectarian Violence

Political and sectarian violence represents a major internal security issue in Pakistan. Political violence, often linked to power struggles, party rivalries, and election-related conflicts, significantly disrupts public order and safety. Sectarian violence, on the other hand, is rooted in religious and sectarian divisions, particularly between Sunni and Shia Muslim communities. Groups driven by extremist ideologies exploit these divisions, instigating violence that has led to loss of life and social harmony. This type of violence not only threatens internal security but also fosters an environment of fear and intolerance, impeding efforts to establish lasting peace.

Ethnic and Linguistic Conflicts

Ethnic and linguistic conflicts also pose a significant threat to Pakistan's internal security. Pakistan's diverse ethnic composition, with major groups including Punjabis, Sindhis, Pashtuns, Baloch, and Mohajirs, has given rise to inter-ethnic tensions and conflicts over resources, political representation, and language-based rights. These conflicts can escalate into violence, destabilizing regions and creating a breeding ground for militancy and insurgencies, as seen in areas like Balochistan.

Urban Crime and Gang Violence

Urban crime, particularly in major cities like Karachi and Lahore, is another serious internal security concern. Organized crime syndicates and street gangs are involved in a range of illegal activities, including drug trafficking, extortion, and targeted killings. These criminal networks often have deep-rooted connections with political parties and law enforcement agencies, making it challenging to curb their activities. This level of crime and violence not only disrupts daily life but also undermines economic stability and social cohesion.

Cyber Security Threats

In the digital age, cyber security threats have become a critical aspect of internal security. As Pakistan becomes increasingly digitized, it faces threats like hacking, data breaches, cyber espionage, and online radicalization. These threats can compromise national security, economic stability, and privacy rights. Despite some steps taken to enhance cyber security, there is a pressing need to further develop the country's digital defence mechanisms and invest in cyber education and awareness to effectively combat these emerging threats.

Terrorism in Pakistan

Terrorism has been a severe challenge to Pakistan's internal security for several decades. The roots of terrorism in the country can be traced back to the 1980s and the aftermath of the Soviet-Afghan War, when Pakistan became a frontline state in the conflict and a breeding ground for militant ideologies.

The landscape of terrorism in Pakistan is varied and complex, comprising diverse forms such as suicide bombings, targeted killings, and sectarian violence. Suicide bombings, often executed by groups like Tehrik-i-Taliban Pakistan (TTP), have caused numerous casualties and significant property damage. Sectarian violence, particularly between Sunni and Shia Muslim communities, has further fueled instability and fear.

Major incidents of terrorism, such as the 2014 Peshawar school massacre, in which more than 140 people, predominantly children, were killed, have deeply scarred the nation, and galvanized the government and military to take decisive action against terrorist outfits. Other notable attacks, such as those on the Marriott Hotel in Islamabad in 2008, and Lahore's Data Darbar shrine in 2010 and again in 2019, underscore the sustained and devastating impact of terrorism on the country.

The impact of terrorism in Pakistan extends far beyond immediate loss of life and property. It has profound implications for the country's economic development, social fabric, and international image. The constant threat of terrorism disrupts economic activities, discourages foreign investment, and places significant strain on the state's resources. It also creates a climate of fear and insecurity, exacerbating social divisions and undermining social cohesion. On a global stage, Pakistan's struggle with terrorism has often been a point of contention, impacting diplomatic relations and shaping international perceptions of the country. Overall, combating terrorism remains a critical aspect of ensuring Pakistan's internal security and sustainable development.

Government Responses and Counter-Terrorism Measures

The Pakistani government, in collaboration with its armed forces and law enforcement agencies, has implemented a series of measures to counter terrorism and enhance internal security. These include large-scale military operations like Zarb-e-Azb and Radd-ul-Fasaad aimed at rooting out militant hideouts in North Waziristan and other volatile regions. There has also been an increased focus on improving intelligence gathering, surveillance, and cyber security capabilities. In the legal sphere, the government has established military courts to expedite terrorism-related cases and strengthened anti-terrorism laws. These measures have resulted in a significant decline in terrorist activities; however, the threat persists, necessitating sustained and comprehensive efforts.

Conclusion

In conclusion, addressing internal security issues and countering terrorism are of paramount importance to ensure the stability, prosperity, and progress of Pakistan. While significant strides have been made, the road ahead requires sustained efforts, social reform, robust law enforcement, and persistent vigilance against emerging threats.

10.2 EXTERNAL SECURITY THREATS AND RELATIONS WITH NEIGHBOURING COUNTRIES

In an increasingly interconnected world, nations must not only contend with internal security issues but also address external security threats. External security threats refer to potential dangers originating outside a nation's borders, such as military aggression, territorial disputes, economic coercion, cyber-attacks, or even transnational issues like climate change, pandemics, and terrorism. For a country like Pakistan, situated at a geopolitically crucial crossroads of South Asia, Central Asia, and the Middle East, managing external security threats is of paramount importance.

The dynamics of international relations significantly influence a nation's external security landscape. Relations with neighbouring countries, in particular, can deeply impact a nation's security, economy, and overall prosperity. For Pakistan, these relations carry immense significance due to historical ties, shared cultural and ethnic affinities, strategic interests, and mutual challenges.

This essay aims to explore the external security threats Pakistan faces and analyse its relations with neighbouring countries, focusing on the unique challenges and opportunities each relationship presents. Through a nuanced exploration of these complex relationships, we aim to shed light on the intertwined paths of security and international diplomacy that Pakistan navigates in its quest for peace and prosperity.

Understanding External Security Threats

External security threats encapsulate a wide array of potential hazards emanating from beyond a nation's borders. The traditional understanding of external security threats primarily includes military aggression and territorial disputes. These threats are often the result of competing national interests, historical animosities, or geopolitical strategies.

However, in the modern world, the scope of external security threats has broadened to include non-traditional threats. These can be cross-border terrorism, transnational organized crime, cyber warfare, economic coercion, and issues of resource scarcity leading to disputes over shared resources like water. Additionally, global issues like climate change, pandemics, and mass migration or refugees can also pose significant security threats due to their potential to disrupt societal stability and exacerbate existing vulnerabilities.

Pakistan, due to its unique geopolitical location and historical context, faces a complex spectrum of external security threats. It is surrounded by neighbours with whom it shares a range of cooperative and conflictual relations. Territorial disputes, most notably over the region of Kashmir with India, have led to repeated conflicts and a persistent state of military alertness.

Additionally, Pakistan grapples with the threat of cross-border terrorism, primarily from its western front, aggravated by the instability in Afghanistan. This threat manifests in various forms, including militant incursions and cross-border bombings. Furthermore, Pakistan's position as a transit route for illegal drug trade and human trafficking between the Golden Crescent and other parts of the world poses unique security and law enforcement challenges.

Issues of resource scarcity also emerge as significant threats, with water disputes with India over shared river systems posing the risk of conflict. The increasing impacts of climate change, which exacerbate water scarcity and lead to environmental migration, further compound these threats.

Thus, Pakistan's external security landscape is shaped by an intricate interplay of traditional and non-traditional threats, deeply embedded in its regional context and historical experiences.

Relations with Neighbouring Countries

India

Pakistan's relations with India have been marked by periods of severe tension and brief instances of rapprochement since their partition in 1947. The central issue of contention is the unresolved territorial dispute over Kashmir. Kashmir remains a flashpoint for military confrontation, having triggered several wars and constant border skirmishes. Apart from this, allegations of state-sponsored terrorism, water disputes, and the lack of meaningful trade relations further strain ties. Despite numerous peace initiatives, sustainable détente remains elusive due to persistent mistrust and geopolitical rivalries.

Afghanistan

Pakistan's relations with Afghanistan are complex and shaped by factors like the Durand Line dispute, the Afghan refugee issue, and the Afghan conflict. Historically, Pakistan has been a significant player in Afghanistan, particularly due to its support for the Afghan Mujahideen during the Soviet-Afghan War and later, its complex ties with the Taliban. The instability in Afghanistan has often translated into security threats for Pakistan, particularly in terms of cross-border terrorism. The recent developments, with the Taliban regaining control, further complicate this relationship.

Iran

Relations with Iran have had their highs and lows, shaped by sectarian dynamics, border security, and regional geopolitics. The two countries share cultural ties, but their relations are often strained due to issues like border security and alleged support for sectarian groups. Moreover, Iran's regional rivalry with Saudi Arabia, a close ally of Pakistan, adds another layer of complexity to the ties.

China

Pakistan enjoys a close and cooperative relationship with China, often referred to as an 'all-weather friendship.' This relationship is anchored in shared strategic interests and strong economic ties, significantly bolstered by the China-Pakistan Economic Corridor (CPEC) project. The CPEC, part of China's ambitious Belt and Road Initiative (BRI), has brought considerable Chinese investment into Pakistan. However, it also raises concerns about debt sustainability and economic sovereignty. Despite these concerns, China remains a crucial ally for Pakistan, offering consistent diplomatic support and robust economic cooperation.

Addressing External Threats

Addressing external security threats is a complex task, requiring a multi-faceted approach that includes diplomacy, military strategy, regional cooperation, and international alliances. Pakistan's strategies to counter external threats and foster healthy relations with its neighbours have evolved over time, incorporating these various dimensions.

Diplomacy has always been a critical tool for Pakistan in managing its international relations. It has sought to engage with its neighbours and the wider international community through diplomatic channels to resolve disputes and build cooperation. For instance, numerous peace initiatives with India, like the Lahore Declaration, highlight Pakistan's diplomatic efforts. Similarly, diplomatic engagement with Afghanistan, especially in the context of the Afghan peace process, demonstrates attempts to build a cooperative regional environment.

In the realm of military strategy, Pakistan has focused on maintaining a credible defence posture to deter external threats. Its nuclear capability is often viewed in this context, as a deterrent, particularly concerning its relations with India.

Regional cooperation forms another vital aspect of Pakistan's approach to external security threats. Pakistan's participation in regional platforms like the South Asian Association for Regional Cooperation (SAARC) and the Economic Cooperation Organization (ECO) demonstrates its commitment to regional dialogue and collaboration. However, regional tensions often undermine these platforms' potential.

The China-Pakistan Economic Corridor (CPEC) is a significant example of strengthening relations through economic cooperation. The project underscores the mutual benefits of cooperation, presenting opportunities for regional integration and development.

Lastly, international alliances have been a consistent feature of Pakistan's strategy. Historically, its alliances with the United States and China have been significant, shaping its security and foreign policies. More recently, its strategic partnership with China has gained prominence, especially with CPEC's development.

Despite these strategies, managing external security threats remains a significant challenge for Pakistan, necessitating constant reassessment and adaptation of its strategies in response to the evolving regional and international landscape.

Conclusion

In conclusion, external security threats and relations with neighbouring countries play a vital role in shaping Pakistan's national security and international standing. This essay has traversed the landscape of external threats facing Pakistan, revealing the complex interplay of traditional and non-traditional security challenges that the nation must address. From territorial disputes to cross-border terrorism and regional tensions, Pakistan's geopolitical position presents a unique confluence of security issues.

The examination of relations with neighbouring countries, including India, Afghanistan, Iran, and China, underlines the importance of diplomatic engagement, conflict resolution, and regional cooperation in maintaining peace and stability. Each relationship carries its dynamics and issues, necessitating tailored approaches.

While Pakistan has employed a combination of strategies to mitigate external threats and foster relations with its neighbours, the journey ahead remains intricate. Future foreign relations will likely depend on regional developments, Pakistan's internal stability, and its ability to negotiate its interests on international platforms. Ultimately, the path to enduring peace and security lies in sustained diplomatic efforts, regional cooperation, and comprehensive security paradigms that address both traditional and non-traditional threats.

10.3 TOWARDS A SAFER PAKISTAN: CHALLENGES AND OPPORTUNITIES

The concept of security transcends its traditional military-based definition, extending to areas that directly influence the daily lives of citizens. In Pakistan, a nation enriched with vast cultural diversity and an intriguing geopolitical position, security emerges as a dynamic and multifaceted concept. Its landscape is marked by a range of challenges, including both internal and external factors such as terrorism, internal conflicts, cross-border tensions, and the looming threat of cyber warfare.

These challenges, however, do not exist in isolation but rather provide the impetus for the nation to critically evaluate its strategies and develop comprehensive solutions. They present opportunities for Pakistan to restructure its approaches, reassess its alliances, strengthen its institutional capabilities, and foster societal resilience. This landscape of challenges is therefore not just an array of threats but also a platform from which Pakistan can advance towards a more secure future.

As we delve into the security issues and discuss the road to a safer Pakistan, it is crucial to acknowledge the intricate interplay of these challenges and opportunities and understand that the path towards a secure nation requires an integrated and balanced approach, involving all facets of security.

Understanding Security in Pakistan

Security, in the context of Pakistan, involves a nuanced and multi-dimensional understanding. Rooted in a socio-political landscape marked by complexity and diversity, it is an intricate blend of internal and external elements. The internal dimension encompasses challenges like political instability, sectarian violence, and economic disparities. Externally, the country navigates complex relationships with its neighbouring countries and global superpowers, addressing territorial disputes, cross-border terrorism, refugee issues, and geostrategic power games.

The spectre of terrorism looms large in Pakistan's security panorama. The nation has grappled with a high incidence of terrorist attacks, affecting its peace and stability. This challenge is both internal, with homegrown extremism, and external, with cross-border terrorism. The conflict in the neighbouring Afghanistan has had a significant spillover effect, with Pakistan bearing the brunt of the refugee crisis and the cross-border militant activities.

Internal conflicts, such as sectarian and ethnic violence, have strained the social fabric and threatened internal stability. These are often deeply intertwined with economic disparities, which exacerbate social tensions and breed discontent.

Externally, the geopolitical position of Pakistan places it in the midst of power dynamics that entail unique security challenges. The country's relationships with India, Afghanistan, Iran, and China, each have their complexities and implications for national security.

Moreover, the rise of cyber threats, given the increasing digitalization of the world, adds another layer to Pakistan's security scenario. Cyber-attacks can compromise national infrastructure, making it an area of growing concern.

Overall, security in Pakistan is a complex tapestry of various interrelated factors. A comprehensive understanding of these elements is crucial for identifying effective strategies to enhance the safety of the nation and to achieve sustainable peace and stability.

Building a Safer Pakistan: Strategies and Approaches

Building a safer Pakistan requires a multi-pronged approach, addressing the security challenges at their roots and developing holistic, sustainable solutions. The nation's response has traditionally involved military action, diplomatic efforts, legal reforms, societal initiatives, and international cooperation, each of which carries its unique significance.

Military action forms the forefront of the immediate response to threats, especially those of a violent nature. The armed forces play a critical role in maintaining the sovereignty and territorial integrity of the country, combating terrorism, and ensuring peace and stability. Operations like Zarb-e-Azb and Radd-ul-Fasaad reflect the Pakistani military's proactive role in countering extremist groups and restoring peace. However, while these operations curtail immediate threats, addressing root causes requires a deeper, more comprehensive approach.

Diplomacy plays a crucial part in resolving international disputes and managing relations with neighbouring countries. The intricate dance of diplomacy, involving negotiations, treaties, and international dialogue, is vital to mitigate external threats and promote regional stability. For instance, dialogue processes with India and negotiations in the Afghanistan peace process reflect attempts at diplomatic resolution.

Legal reforms, such as strengthening laws against terrorism, enhancing the judicial process for swift and fair trials, and ensuring rule of law, are essential to address security challenges. These reforms can also include laws to counter hate speech and incitement to violence, thus addressing some root causes of unrest.

Societal initiatives include efforts at the community level to foster unity and counter divisive narratives. Educational programs that promote tolerance, inclusion, and critical thinking can help shape a society resilient to extremist ideologies. Furthermore, socio-economic development initiatives, especially in marginalized areas, can address grievances that often fuel unrest.

International cooperation is key in dealing with security challenges, especially those with cross-border implications. Collaborative efforts, such as intelligence sharing, joint operations against terrorist networks, and mutual legal assistance, can be effective strategies. Additionally, Pakistan's active role in global counter-terrorism frameworks and its cooperation with the UN and other international bodies reflect the importance of this aspect.

However, while these strategies are crucial, they are often reactive rather than proactive. For a safer Pakistan, it is imperative to shift from a largely reactive security paradigm to a more proactive and preventative one. This involves addressing the root causes of insecurity, including political, socio-economic, and ideological factors. It also means investing in human security - education, health, and social welfare - to build a resilient society that can resist the lures of extremism and violence.

Building a safer Pakistan is no small task. It requires the concerted efforts of all sectors of society, from the government to the general public, and a comprehensive, long-term vision. However, the trials and tribulations the country has undergone have equipped it with valuable lessons that, if heeded, can guide the way towards a future marked by peace and security.

Conclusion

In conclusion, navigating the complex security landscape of Pakistan presents significant challenges, both internal and external. Terrorism, internal conflicts, and external threats from neighbouring countries are multifaceted issues deeply intertwined with socio-political dynamics. However, acknowledging the complexity of these challenges is the first step towards formulating effective responses.

Pakistan's approach to security, encompassing military action, diplomacy, legal reforms, societal initiatives, and international cooperation, signifies a comprehensive response to these threats. Yet, the path to a safer Pakistan hinge on a shift from reactive to proactive measures, addressing the root causes of insecurity, and investing in human security, ultimately building a society resilient to extremist ideologies and violence.

The journey towards a safer Pakistan is filled with trials, but also brimming with opportunities. With concerted effort, resilience, and vision, Pakistan can navigate its security challenges and build a future characterized by peace, stability, and prosperity. The trials of the past and present can forge a nation better prepared and fortified against future challenges, advancing steadily towards a safer tomorrow.

11. THE ROAD TO SUCCESS

11.1 ENVISIONING A PROSPEROUS PAKISTAN

Prosperity, a term often associated with wealth and economic success, encompasses a much wider spectrum in the context of a nation. For a country like Pakistan, prosperity implies not just financial stability, but also progress in social, political, environmental, and human developmental domains. It's a multidimensional concept that speaks to the quality of life, opportunities, and well-being of its citizens.

Pakistan, as a country, holds immense potential for prosperity. Boasting the fifth-largest population in the world, it is a country that is abundant with human capital. More than 60% of Pakistan's population is under the age of 30, indicating a strong demographic dividend that, if properly harnessed, can play a crucial role in driving the country's development and prosperity.

In addition to its human capital, Pakistan's geographical location adds another layer to its potential. Positioned at the crossroads of South Asia, Central Asia, and the Middle East, it has the capability to emerge as a major trade and energy corridor. This strategic location provides Pakistan with a unique opportunity to enhance its regional connectivity and reap economic benefits.

Moreover, Pakistan is blessed with diverse natural resources that contribute to its potential for prosperity. It has vast agricultural land, significant reserves of minerals and metals, and a sizable amount of fresh water sources. If sustainably managed, these resources can support a wide range of economic activities and boost Pakistan's prosperity.

However, it's important to recognize that potential does not automatically translate into prosperity. It requires the right policies, investments, and a conducive environment to turn this potential into actual progress. The journey towards prosperity, while filled with challenges, can also lead to the transformation of Pakistan into a more resilient, equitable, and prosperous nation. As we delve into this essay, we will further explore what prosperity entails, the areas where Pakistan holds potential, and the pathways that can lead the country towards a prosperous future.

Understanding Prosperity

Prosperity is an intricate concept that extends beyond mere financial or economic wealth. It embodies several dimensions including economic growth, social equality, political stability, environmental sustainability, and human development. Each of these components intertwines to create a holistic view of a nation's prosperity.

Economic Growth

The backbone of prosperity lies in a strong and stable economy. Economic growth is measured through indicators like Gross Domestic Product (GDP), per capita income, employment rates, and levels of trade. A prosperous nation has a robust economy that ensures employment opportunities, income security, and sustainable growth. Pakistan, with its burgeoning population and strategic geographical location, has immense potential for economic growth. However, persistent challenges such as energy shortages, corruption, and inefficient tax collection systems have constrained its economic progress.

Social Equality

A prosperous nation is one that upholds principles of equality and fairness. It ensures that wealth and opportunities are evenly distributed among its citizens, regardless of their social, economic, or ethnic backgrounds. In the case of Pakistan, strides have been made to promote social equality, but disparities persist, as evidenced by gaps in income, education, and health outcomes across different social strata.

Political Stability

This refers to the level of predictability, tranquillity, and functionality of political institutions and processes within a country. Political stability provides an enabling environment for economic growth, social development, and overall prosperity. Pakistan's political landscape, though vibrant, has been marked by periods of instability which have posed challenges to its path to prosperity.

Environmental Sustainability

In an era of rapid environmental degradation and climate change, a prosperous nation is one that values and protects its environment. This includes sustainable management of natural resources, climate change mitigation and adaptation, and preservation of biodiversity. While Pakistan is endowed with rich natural resources, it is also among the countries most vulnerable to climate change, highlighting the need for increased efforts towards environmental sustainability.

Human Development

Last but not least, prosperity hinges on human development, which entails factors such as education, health, and standard of living. The Human Development Index (HDI) is a commonly used measure of this aspect. Despite improvements over the years, Pakistan still lags behind on various human development indicators, including literacy rates, health services, and gender equality.

In summary, prosperity is a multidimensional concept that requires a balanced and holistic approach. For Pakistan to reach its full potential of prosperity, it needs to address these diverse aspects effectively and efficiently. In the following sections, we will further delve into Pakistan's potential and the pathways that can guide it towards prosperity.

Areas of Potential

Economic Development

Pakistan's economic potential is significant, stemming from diverse sectors. Its agriculture sector, a traditional cornerstone of the economy, holds vast potential for growth. Modernization and technological innovations in farming techniques can boost productivity and tackle food security issues.

The industrial sector, including manufacturing and mining, has been the engine of economic growth in many developed nations. In Pakistan, industries like textiles, automotive, construction, and technology have enormous potential for expansion and job creation. However, it requires improvements in infrastructure, regulatory policies, and vocational training.

The services sector is another area of significant potential. It encompasses a wide range of activities including retail, telecommunications, information technology, finance, and tourism. Particularly, the burgeoning IT industry, driven by a young and tech-savvy population, can be a major growth driver for Pakistan.

Moreover, embracing innovation and technology across all sectors can catalyse economic development. With advancements in digital technologies, opportunities for e-commerce, digital finance, and tech start-ups are rising, promising a more dynamic and inclusive economy.

Social Development

Social development is fundamental to a prosperous Pakistan. In the education sector, expanding access to quality education, particularly for girls and marginalized communities, is key to building a skilled workforce and promoting social equity. Healthcare is another critical domain. Strengthening public health infrastructure, enhancing access to affordable healthcare services, and improving health outcomes are crucial steps towards social development. These measures not only improve citizens' wellbeing but also contribute to economic productivity.

Promoting gender equality can also unleash enormous social and economic potential. This involves empowering women in various facets of life, including education, employment, and decision-making roles. Simultaneously, social protection programs for the vulnerable, like the Benazir Income Support Programme, are vital in reducing poverty and inequality.

Environmental Sustainability

Pakistan is endowed with abundant natural resources and has significant potential in harnessing these sustainably. Effective management of water resources, forests, and minerals can contribute to economic growth while maintaining environmental balance.

Renewable energy, especially solar and wind energy, presents an excellent opportunity for Pakistan. Investing in these technologies can address energy shortages, reduce dependence on imported fuels, and mitigate greenhouse gas emissions.

Further, given Pakistan's vulnerability to climate change, building climate resilience is critical. This entails adapting agricultural practices, improving water management, and developing infrastructure that can withstand extreme weather events.

Overall, these areas present immense potential for fostering a prosperous Pakistan. However, realizing this potential requires effective policies, robust institutions, international cooperation, and most importantly, the collective will of the Pakistani people.

Pathways to Prosperity

Governance and Institutional Reforms

Good governance is crucial to fostering prosperity. This starts with upholding the rule of law, which ensures that all individuals and institutions are accountable, thereby promoting trust in the state and facilitating economic transactions. Efforts should be made to strengthen the judicial system, improve law enforcement, and protect human rights.

Transparency is another key aspect of governance. It helps to prevent corruption, which erodes public resources and undermines economic development. Therefore, enhancing the transparency of government operations, improving the accountability of public officials, and empowering watchdog institutions are necessary steps.

Moreover, administrative efficiency needs to be improved. This involves reforms to streamline bureaucratic processes, adopt digital technologies, and enhance the capacity of public servants. Such reforms can make public services more accessible and effective, which in turn can foster social equity and economic growth.

Investment in Human Capital

Investing in human capital is fundamental to achieving prosperity. Education is at the core of this. Expanding access to quality education, modernizing curricula, and emphasizing skill development can prepare the workforce for the demands of the modern economy.

Health is another key area. Enhancing the quality and accessibility of healthcare services, prioritizing preventive care, and addressing public health challenges like malnutrition and infectious diseases can improve the health and productivity of the population.

Moreover, social protection programs should be expanded to support the most vulnerable. These programs can help alleviate poverty, reduce inequality, and foster social cohesion. They can include cash transfers, public works programs, and social insurance.

Sustainable and Inclusive Economic Policies

Prosperity also requires sustainable and inclusive economic policies. Economic diversification is crucial to reduce dependence on a few sectors and create a resilient economy. This involves promoting entrepreneurship, supporting small and medium enterprises, and investing in research and development.

Job creation is another key aspect. Strategies to stimulate job growth can include improving the business environment, promoting industries with high employment potential, and implementing active labour market policies.

Moreover, social safety nets are important to protect the vulnerable and ensure that economic growth benefits all segments of society. These can include unemployment benefits, old-age pensions, and child support grants.

Lastly, environmental sustainability needs to be incorporated into economic policies. This involves promoting green technologies, preserving natural resources, and adopting climate change mitigation and adaptation strategies. Such measures not only protect the environment but also provide opportunities for green growth and job creation.

Role of National and International Stakeholders

The journey towards a prosperous Pakistan is a collective endeavour, involving numerous national and international stakeholders.

On the national level, the government plays a pivotal role through policymaking and implementing public services. It should steer reforms for good governance, invest in human capital, and promote sustainable economic policies. The private sector, meanwhile, is crucial for job creation, innovation, and economic growth. Companies should embrace corporate social responsibility, invest in employee development, and adopt sustainable business practices. Civil society, including NGOs, academia, and the media, can advocate for social issues, contribute to policy debates, and hold public and private institutions accountable.

International partners also play a significant role. Bilateral and multilateral donors can provide financial and technical assistance to support Pakistan's development programs. International NGOs can offer expertise and implement projects in areas such as education, health, and environment. Multinational corporations can invest in Pakistan's economy, creating jobs and transferring technology.

In this shared endeavour, collaboration, dialogue, and partnership among all these stakeholders are crucial to navigate the complexities of development and move Pakistan towards prosperity.

Conclusion

In conclusion, envisioning a prosperous Pakistan is not a mere daydream but a plausible reality within reach. This nation, blessed with abundant resources, a strategic location, and a dynamic youthful population, has substantial potential for economic, social, and environmental prosperity. From strengthening governance and institutional frameworks to investing in human capital and promoting sustainable economic policies, the pathways to prosperity are diverse and interconnected. With the collaborative efforts of various national and international stakeholders, Pakistan can turn the tide of challenges into opportunities. The journey towards prosperity may be long and complex, but the future of Pakistan holds promise and hope.

11.2 STRATEGIES AND SOLUTIONS FOR OVERCOMING HURDLES

The path to national progress for any country is invariably fraught with hurdles and challenges. In the case of Pakistan, a complex web of interrelated obstacles presents a multifaceted predicament that demands nuanced understanding and strategic action. These hurdles range from economic instability to social inequalities, from environmental challenges to governance issues.

Economic instability, characterized by factors such as inflation, unemployment, and budget deficits, has consistently stunted Pakistan's growth potential. Simultaneously, deeply entrenched social inequalities – spanning gender, class, and regional divides – have perpetuated systemic injustice and hindered comprehensive national development. Environmental challenges, too, pose significant threats. Given Pakistan's high vulnerability to climate change, problems like water scarcity, pollution, and natural disasters present critical obstacles to sustainable development. Lastly, governance issues, including corruption, weak rule of law, and institutional inefficiency, have often impeded effective policy implementation and service delivery.

Each of these hurdles is a considerable impediment on its own, but their interlinked nature compounds their impact, making it all the more important to devise effective strategies and solutions. The task is undeniably complex but absolutely vital to ensure Pakistan's steady journey towards sustainable and inclusive growth. Recognizing and understanding these hurdles is the first step; the subsequent and perhaps more important stage is identifying and implementing potent solutions to overcome them. This discourse is not just about diagnosing Pakistan's challenges but, crucially, about charting a feasible course to surmount these obstacles and foster national progress.

Understanding the Hurdles

Economic Instability

Pakistan's economic landscape is riddled with instability, posing significant hurdles to sustainable growth. High inflation rates, coupled with low GDP growth, generate a tumultuous economic climate that hinders investment and enterprise development. The pervasive issue of unemployment, particularly among the youth, adds to the socioeconomic strain. Moreover, Pakistan's large fiscal deficits, exacerbated by substantial debt servicing, limit the government's capacity to invest in critical sectors such as education, health, and infrastructure. This economic volatility not only impedes immediate growth prospects but also threatens long-term stability and prosperity.

Social Inequalities

Pakistan's path to progress is significantly impeded by deep-seated social inequalities. Disparities based on class, gender, and regional divisions hamper the realization of social justice and inclusive growth. Gender inequality, manifested in the disparities in education, employment, and representation in public life, is particularly concerning. Economic disparities, marked by widespread poverty and wealth concentration, further accentuate social divisions. Additionally, regional inequalities, expressed in uneven development and resource allocation among provinces, contribute to social discontent and political instability.

Environmental Challenges

As one of the most climate-vulnerable countries, Pakistan faces serious environmental challenges that pose hurdles to sustainable development. Issues like water scarcity, air and water pollution, deforestation, and loss of biodiversity are increasingly urgent. The country also grapples with the heightened risk of natural disasters, such as floods and droughts, exacerbated by climate change. These environmental issues not only pose a direct threat to human lives and livelihoods but also impact economic growth and social stability.

Governance Issues

Governance issues pose significant hurdles to Pakistan's progress. These encompass corruption, a weak rule of law, and inefficient public institutions. Corruption, whether in public or private sectors, undermines trust in institutions and hampers economic development. The weak rule of law and a lack of accountability contribute to social unrest and insecurity. Inefficiencies in public institutions impede the delivery of essential services like health, education, and justice. These governance challenges weaken the state's capacity to address other hurdles, creating a vicious cycle that undermines overall national progress.

Strategies and Solutions

Solutions for Economic Instability

Addressing economic instability in Pakistan necessitates a multi-faceted strategy. Fundamental to this is fiscal discipline, aimed at reducing public debt and maintaining a sustainable deficit level. Tax reforms, geared towards broadening the tax base and enhancing collection efficiency, can enhance government revenue and create fiscal space for public investment. Additionally, structural reforms are needed to enhance the competitiveness of Pakistan's economy. This includes investment in infrastructure, boosting agricultural productivity, and promoting industrialization and innovation. Job creation, especially for the youth, is also critical and can be achieved through supporting small and medium-sized enterprises (SMEs) and fostering a conducive environment for entrepreneurship. Finally, strengthening social safety nets can protect the most vulnerable from economic shocks and contribute to social stability.

Solutions for Social Inequalities

Tackling social inequalities requires concerted efforts across various domains. Expanding access to quality education and health services is critical to reducing income inequalities and promoting social mobility. Gender equality should be pursued through legislative measures against gender-based discrimination, initiatives to increase women's participation in economic and public life, and interventions to change societal attitudes. To address regional disparities, a balanced development strategy is needed that ensures fair resource allocation and fosters local economic development across all provinces. Moreover, social protection policies should be strengthened to safeguard the rights of the most vulnerable groups, including the poor, women, minorities, and the differently abled.

Solutions for Environmental Challenges

Overcoming environmental challenges calls for a robust, comprehensive, and proactive approach. This includes strengthening environmental governance through effective regulation and enforcement of environmental standards. Efforts should be made to promote sustainable agricultural practices, efficient water use, and conservation of biodiversity. There should be a transition towards renewable and cleaner energy sources to mitigate air pollution and reduce carbon emissions. Climate change adaptation and mitigation strategies are needed, encompassing disaster risk reduction, climate-resilient infrastructure, and community-level resilience building.

Importantly, environmental education and awareness-raising can foster a culture of environmental stewardship and drive behavioural changes at the individual and community levels.

Solutions for Governance Issues

Addressing governance issues in Pakistan requires both institutional reforms and a change in political culture. Corruption can be tackled through strengthening accountability mechanisms, promoting transparency, and enforcing strict penalties. Judicial and police reforms are needed to strengthen the rule of law and ensure justice. Public sector efficiency can be enhanced through administrative reforms, capacity building, and leveraging technology for better service delivery. Further, decentralization of power can enhance local governance and make it more responsive to community needs. Importantly, cultivating a political culture of integrity, public service, and civic responsibility is necessary to drive these reforms and ensure their sustainability. Ultimately, good governance is the linchpin that can enable progress across all other domains.

Role of Various Stakeholders

The journey towards overcoming Pakistan's hurdles is one that calls for the collective effort of multiple stakeholders, each playing a unique and pivotal role.

The government, being the primary actor in governance, holds the responsibility for policymaking, regulation, and service delivery. It is tasked with driving the necessary reforms in areas such as economic policy, social protection, environmental regulation, and public sector management. Moreover, it plays a crucial role in mobilizing resources, both domestically and from international sources, to invest in critical areas such as infrastructure, education, healthcare, and climate resilience.

The private sector's role is essential in driving economic growth, innovation, and job creation. It has the potential to bring about economic stability through investment, industrial growth, and the provision of goods and services. Moreover, through corporate social responsibility initiatives, businesses can contribute to addressing social and environmental challenges.

Civil society, encompassing non-governmental organizations, community groups, and citizens, plays a key role in advocating for rights, holding the government accountable, and providing services where government capacity is lacking. Through awareness-raising, advocacy, and grassroots action, civil society can drive societal transformation towards greater equity and sustainability.

International organizations, such as the United Nations, World Bank, and bilateral aid agencies, are key partners in Pakistan's development journey. They provide financial and technical assistance, support policy reforms, and facilitate knowledge sharing and capacity building.

Collaboration and synergy among these stakeholders can effectively implement the strategies and solutions identified and significantly contribute to overcoming Pakistan's hurdles.

Conclusion

As we navigate through the labyrinth of complexities that Pakistan faces, it becomes evident that these hurdles - economic instability, social inequalities, environmental challenges, and governance issues - are intricately interwoven. These issues cannot be examined or resolved in isolation; rather, they demand comprehensive strategies and concerted efforts.

To combat economic instability, measures such as diversification of economy, investment in human capital, and trade liberalization hold promise. For tackling social inequalities, the implementation of inclusive policies, strengthening of social safety nets, and promotion of gender equality are crucial. To mitigate environmental challenges, a blend of sustainable practices, innovative technologies, and regulatory measures are required. To address governance issues, the enforcement of rule of law, eradication of corruption, and improvement of public services are key.

We must also acknowledge the critical roles that various stakeholders play. The government, as a policymaker and regulator; the private sector, as an engine of growth; civil society, as a watchdog and advocate; and international organizations, as partners in development. Their collective efforts can lead to a transformational change in Pakistan's landscape.

Throughout this discourse, it is essential to base our understanding and approach on evidence, learning from successful case studies, and data-driven insights. This would lend credibility and effectiveness to our strategies and solutions.

In conclusion, while the hurdles that Pakistan faces are significant, they are not insurmountable. By leveraging the right strategies, nurturing cooperation among stakeholders, and fostering a culture of resilience and innovation, a prosperous future for Pakistan is indeed attainable.

11.3 THE ROLE OF GLOBAL PARTNERSHIPS IN PAKISTAN'S PROGRESS

In the intricate web of contemporary international relations, global partnerships have emerged as a crucial factor driving national development and progress. From fostering economic growth and technological innovation to addressing complex challenges such as climate change and public health crises, global collaborations hold significant potential. For countries like Pakistan, strategically positioned and home to a diverse array of resources, these partnerships are not just beneficial—they are essential. This essay will explore the role and importance of global partnerships in Pakistan's progress, underlining how these alliances have shaped and will continue to Mold the country's journey towards prosperity.

Understanding Global Partnerships

Global partnerships represent a commitment to collaborative efforts that cross national boundaries, aimed at achieving common objectives such as economic prosperity, sustainable development, peace, and security, among others. They operate on the principles of shared values, mutual respect, and common interests, and involve a multitude of stakeholders including nations, international organizations, non-governmental organizations, and even private sector entities.

For example, the United Nations, an emblem of global partnership, unites 193 countries towards maintaining international peace and security, advancing human rights, and promoting sustainable development. Similarly, the World Bank, another significant global entity, works towards reducing poverty and promoting shared prosperity by providing financial and technical assistance to developing countries.

Regional trade organizations, like the Association of Southeast Asian Nations (ASEAN) or the South Asian Association for Regional Cooperation (SAARC), are other examples of partnerships where neighbouring countries unite to promote regional trade and cooperation, political stability, and socio-cultural exchange. These entities exemplify the functioning and potential of global partnerships and the immense value they can bring to individual member states and the global community at large.

Global Partnerships and Pakistan

Historical Perspective

Pakistan's international relations and its engagement in global partnerships has a rich and dynamic history. Since its independence in 1947, Pakistan has been an active participant in numerous international alliances, shaping both its domestic developments and its role on the global stage.

Pakistan joined the United Nations immediately after its inception and has been a significant contributor to UN peacekeeping missions globally. During the Cold War era, Pakistan allied itself with the United States and became a member of the Southeast Asia Treaty Organization (SEATO) and Central Treaty Organization (CENTO), primarily aimed at countering the spread of communism.

On the economic front, Pakistan became a member of the International Monetary Fund and the World Bank in 1950. These organizations have played a vital role in Pakistan's economic development through financial assistance and technical expertise.

In the regional context, Pakistan, along with other South Asian countries, established the South Asian Association for Regional Cooperation (SAARC) to promote economic and regional integration.

Current Global Partnerships

In the contemporary world, Pakistan continues to engage in multiple global partnerships. Its relationship with China has significantly intensified with the China-Pakistan Economic Corridor (CPEC), a project under China's ambitious Belt and Road Initiative. This multi-billion-dollar project aims to connect Gwadar Port in southwestern Pakistan with China's northwestern region of Xinjiang, fostering economic growth and regional connectivity.

Pakistan also maintains strategic partnerships with the United States, particularly focusing on security and counterterrorism. Besides, it engages with the European Union, the United Kingdom, and other Western countries on trade, development assistance, and human rights issues.

Regionally, Pakistan is an active member of the SAARC and the Economic Cooperation Organization (ECO), promoting regional integration, trade liberalization, and economic cooperation. It is also an observer state in the Shanghai Cooperation Organization (SCO), fostering closer relations with Central Asian countries.

Additionally, Pakistan engages with international financial institutions like the World Bank, IMF, and Asian Development Bank for economic development and reform programs. Furthermore, it participates in global initiatives addressing climate change, sustainable development, and peacekeeping under the UN framework.

These partnerships and alliances demonstrate Pakistan's continued engagement with the global community, shaping its path towards a prosperous and secure future.

The Impact of Global Partnerships on Pakistan's Progress

Global partnerships have had substantial impacts on various sectors in Pakistan, stimulating progress and development. For instance, collaborations with international organizations like the World Bank and the Asian Development Bank have led to numerous projects aimed at strengthening infrastructure, improving education and healthcare, and boosting economic growth.

In the realm of security, partnerships with countries like the United States have been instrumental in enhancing counter-terrorism capabilities and promoting regional stability. On the technology front, collaborations with countries like China have helped foster advancements in telecommunications and information technology, significantly contributing to the digitalization of Pakistan's economy.

Furthermore, partnerships with global health organizations have supported the improvement of health services and disease control initiatives in Pakistan. Lastly, in the education sector, collaborations with international educational institutions and development organizations have helped to enhance educational access and quality, contributing to human capital development.

In sum, global partnerships have provided Pakistan with crucial support and resources to address its challenges and drive its progress across various sectors.

Conclusion

In conclusion, global partnerships have been, and continue to be, integral to Pakistan's progress. They have influenced various sectors, driving advancements in infrastructure, education, healthcare, and security. As Pakistan continues to navigate its path to development, these partnerships will remain vital, offering the potential to catalyse further growth, progress, and prosperity.

12. CONCLUSION

12.1 REFLECTING ON PAKISTAN'S UNVEILED POTENTIAL: A SUMMARY

In the chapters preceding this, we have undertaken a detailed journey through the complexities and contrasts that illustrate Pakistan's journey. The nation stands as a study in contrasts, where opulence brushes shoulders with scarcity, where the quest for peace is an ongoing struggle against internal and external disturbances, and where advancements are often shadowed by setbacks. This in-depth analysis has allowed us to fully comprehend the influences and interactions that mold Pakistan's progress.

This book seeks to go beyond merely cataloging the nation's struggles and achievements. It is an invitation to understand the depth and breadth of Pakistan's history and current state to illuminate a pathway toward a brighter, more prosperous future. We have investigated the intricate socio-economic and political weave of Pakistan, examining how the combined threads of advancement and challenges form the nation's unique identity.

As we draw our exploration to a close, it is time to step back and consider the broader picture. A landscape where economic growth occurs alongside enduring need, where every victory in enhancing security is hard-won against persistent threats, and where for every technological or educational leap forward, there may be a stumble due to deep-rooted social and economic barriers. The following pages offer a succinct overview of this complex investigation.

Review of the Complex Contrasts

We began by analyzing the contrast of economic growth amid widespread poverty, laying bare the economic core of Pakistan. Despite abundant resources and strategic positioning, economic fluctuation, and disparity continue. Structural shortcomings, governance issues, and economic policies were scrutinized, juxtaposed with potential sectors for growth and human resource development. We contended that equitable economic strategies and governance refinement are crucial for converting these contrasts into a vehicle for consistent economic growth.

Turning to national security, despite a strong military presence, Pakistan faces multifarious security issues. The roots of these issues, their implications for national stability, and Pakistan's multifaceted counter-strategies were discussed, concluding that a holistic approach is imperative for securing peace and stability.

In discussing the contrast between development and regression, we recognized advancements in education and health, countered by social inequalities and environmental concerns. We identified actionable strategies, stressing the need for engagement from all societal sectors. The potential for substantial progress with effective implementation of these strategies was underlined.

The final contrast considered Pakistan's role in international alliances amidst domestic intricacies. Historical and contemporary partnerships and their influence on various sectors were explored, concluding that international relationships are crucial for overcoming domestic issues and propelling development.

Reflections on the Complex Contrasts

Reflecting on these complexities reveals a web of interdependencies that provide profound insight into Pakistan's society, politics, economy, and culture. Each contrast is a thread in the national fabric, illustrating the intricacies of Pakistan's path to progress.

The contrast between wealth and want underscores the urgent need for inclusive growth. Security issues in the limelight necessitate comprehensive solutions, incorporating military, political, and social strategies. The developmental ebb and flow emphasize the importance of consistent policy and institutional integrity. The balance between national aspirations and global dynamics underlines the significance of international cooperation for national advancement.

Recognizing these complexities is key to portraying a complete picture of Pakistan's development, capturing its challenges, opportunities, and potential. They illuminate the past and guide us towards a more prosperous and secure future. Translating these contrasts from challenges to successes is central to envisioning and achieving a better tomorrow for Pakistan.

Pathways Forward

Looking ahead, Pakistan's journey towards reconciling its contrasts involves multi-faceted, concerted action. The country must harness economic policies that promote shared growth, bolster human capital, and embrace innovation. Addressing security requires reinforcing defense mechanisms, advancing peace initiatives, and nurturing regional and international diplomacy. Environmental sustainability and democratic governance are pillars for enduring prosperity.

Globally, Pakistan must further develop and utilize strategic partnerships to reinforce national development. Seizing every chance to incorporate global insights, resources, and participation on the world stage will be vital.

In essence, Pakistan's route to success lies in converting its contrasts into potential, its obstacles into opportunities, and the wisdom gained from its past into a blueprint for a thriving and secure future.

Conclusion

"Pakistan Unveiled: A Study of Dichotomies and Challenges"

Thus concludes with a reinforcement of the pivotal role of understanding and addressing the nation's intricate contrasts for sustainable advancement. The vision of a flourishing, secure, and resilient Pakistan is within reach, contingent upon our collective resolve, diligence, and unwavering optimism for progress.

Printed and Bound by *Passive Printers* - www.passiveprinters.com
Printing press that offers Print on Demand (POD) Facility.
Printed in The Islamic Republic of Pakistan.

Printed in Great Britain
by Amazon

43251287R10118